YOUCAT

Confirmation course
Handbook

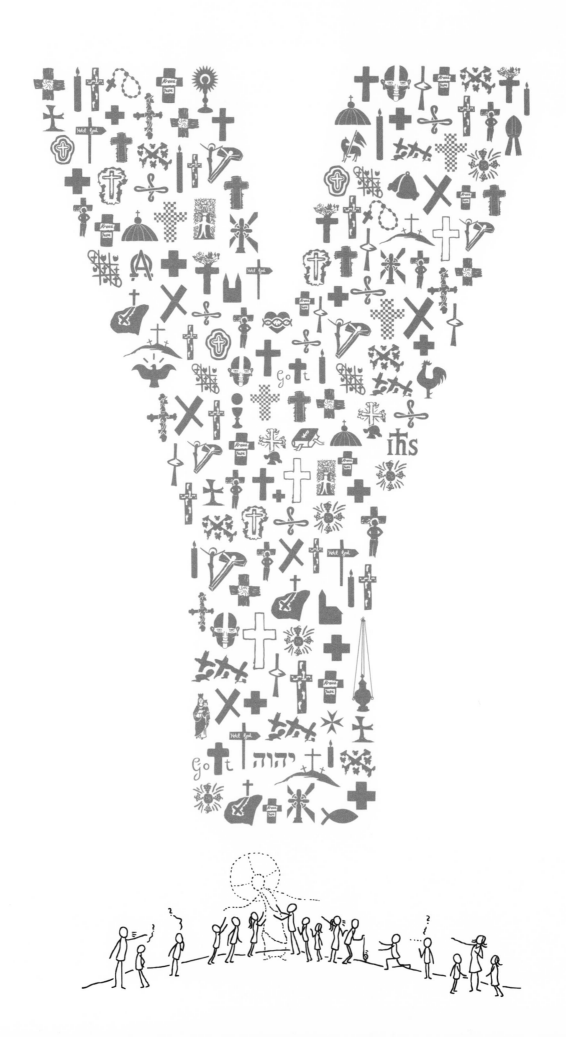

YOUCAT

Confirmation course
Handbook

Edited by
Nils Baer
in collaboration with the
YOUCAT Team, Augsburg

Translated by Frank Davidson

IGNATIUS PRESS   SAN FRANCISCO

IMPRIMATUR PENDING

Original German Edition:
Der YOUCAT Firmkurs: Handbuch
© 2012 by Sankt Ulrich Verlag GmbH, Augsburg

Cover design, layout, illustrations, and typesetting: Alexander von Lengerke, Cologne
Overall production: Auer Buch + Medien GmbH, Donauwörth

The trademark YOUCAT is used with the kind permission of the publisher of YOUCAT—Youth Catechism of the Catholic Church www.youcat.org

© 2014 by Ignatius Press, San Francisco
All rights reserved
ISBN 978-1-58617-836-9
Printed in the United States of America ♾

20 19 18 17 16 15 14 13 12 11 10 9 8 7 6 5 4 3

Contents

Foreword

> "The Church is alive, and she is young", Pope Benedict has told us. And in YOUCAT we deliberately adopt this youthful and informal manner—toward you, the group leader, as well. This should not be misunderstood as presumption or a lack of respect, however.

Ever since the YOUCAT began its triumphant progress, leading to the more than 2.5 million copies that have now been printed, the most frequent question we have encountered has not been "Is the Pope really infallible?" or "What has the Church got against condoms?", but "When are you going to get around to producing a YOUCAT Confirmation course?" Well, here it is.

"Young people are not so superficial", writes the Pope in his foreword to the YOUCAT. It's true. They want to know what they believe. And so this course is shaped around the fundamental content of our faith. But because this can sometimes be quite tough going, we have made sure to leave room for a little fun as well.

The course consists of the YOUCAT Confirmation course book for the students and the handbook you are now reading. The two books belong together and complement each other. The two books follow the same twelve steps leading to Confirmation—and both books refer to the same key passages in the Bible and in the YOUCAT.

The Confirmation course book is addressed directly to the young people in your Confirmation group and explains to them in an attractive manner, as though in a novel of twelve chapters, what the Confirmation course is all about.

In the handbook you will find fully planned lessons, relating directly to the twelve chapters in the course book. In addition, for each chapter there is a brief article giving the theological basis, which should help to provide you, as the Confirmation group leader, with the necessary background knowledge. Overall, then, an integrated network results, comprising the YOUCAT, the Bible, the course book, this handbook, and your own Confirmation lessons—since all these things will always be interrelated.

How you can work with this handbook

Size of the group
In preparing the lessons, we envisaged a group of around eight to ten Confirmation candidates, who would regularly meet together as a group.

Basic resources
The basic resources for this Confirmation course will include a Bible and a copy of the YOUCAT.

YOUCAT Confirmation course material
We have already prepared a good deal of material for you in advance, in the shape of cards, pictures, and worksheets. You will find them at the end of each lesson. Printable copies of all course materials available online at youcat confirmation.com. Click on "PDF Resources" and go to the desired lesson for worksheets. So you have only to copy or cut out these pages as you need them.

Media and other resources
For a number of the lessons, you will need additional material that, for practical and legal reasons, we cannot simply include—for example, when we suggest watching a film or making a candle.

Preparation
For this reason it is quite important that you prepare the lesson well in advance. This means that you read through the material, look up the suggested Bible texts and YOUCAT passages, and, of course, get hold of the necessary materials. If you discover only twenty minutes before the lesson begins that you need ten white candles and wax sheets in nine different colors, then things are likely to get a little pressured.

Format of the handbook

Theological basis

The handbook is arranged in such a way that for each topic you will first of all find an introduction, giving you general information about the topic. Not everything that is explained there will be found later in the suggested lesson plans. The "theological basis" section is there to give you a basic idea of what this particular topic is about.

Suggested lesson plans

The introduction is usually followed by two suggestions about how you can approach the topic in practice with your group. You can then choose from the two plans the one best suited to your group. Theological information that is absolutely essential in the course of this lesson will once again be briefly explained here.

Materials

At the end of each lesson, you will find the materials we have already prepared for you. All you have to do is photocopy it or, if you prefer, cut it out. These materials are also available at youcatconfirmation.com.

Confirmation course book

This handbook for you, as the catechist, is complemented by the YOUCAT Confirmation course book for your students. All the topics are explained there in an entertaining way and are sometimes examined from a quite different aspect. It therefore makes sense for you, the catechist, to take a look at the course book as well in preparing for each lesson. Maybe you will come up with a few additional good ideas yourself as a result.

Signs and symbols

B → 1 Cor 9:24–27   Bible reference
Y → 203   reference to YOUCAT

Most of the lessons in the YOUCAT Confirmation course offer a choice of two different levels of difficulty in order to take different age groups into account. You must decide here which is more appropriate to your group.

 fairly simple,   rather more challenging   somewhere in between.

Why you are important for this Confirmation course

This handbook provides you with a large fund of background information, ideas, and materials to support you in your work as leader of a Confirmation group.
However, you are more important than all these materials.

You are the face of the Church

That's because you are the face of the Confirmation course for your students and, as a result, often the face of the Church as well. Do not underestimate your influence in this regard. If you present your faith credibly and openly in these lessons, this will make a big impression on your young people. Even when they are perhaps not always immediately convinced by the teachings of the Church.

Take Jesus on board with you

If you're starting to think that's a big responsibility to place on your shoulders, then of course you're right. That's why you shouldn't have to bear it alone. Take Jesus on board with you. After all, the whole thing is about his Church. And without him, it won't succeed in any case.

That's why it also makes sense for you to pray regularly for your Confirmation group. Not only when things aren't going so well, but also when everything is working out beautifully.

Renew your own faith

On this Confirmation course you are the one who is meant to be guiding your young people a few steps farther forward on their path to Jesus. So it is a good idea for you to renew or strengthen your own faith beforehand. A good way of doing so is through regularly available courses in the Catholic faith. Another way to gain a deeper understanding is to get together with other catechists and use YOUCAT to prepare together for the upcoming lessons; then you can exchange ideas among yourselves about the topics to be discussed.

What is important in every lesson

BIBLE SESSION, **YOUCAT SESSION**, and **DISCUSSION** should be part of every lesson. The points you generally need to keep in mind are summarized briefly below:

BIBLE SESSION
All the students should have the text in front of them

In the Bible session, you should read the relevant text from the Bible together. Every student should have a Bible in hand, ideally the same version. An excellent and readily available version is the second Catholic edition of the Revised Standard Version.

Reading together

The best approach is for one of the students to read the relevant text out loud, while the others follow the reading quietly in their own Bibles. A good person to choose here would be someone who is otherwise rather quiet, in order to get him involved. We strongly advise against such games as: "Everyone reads a sentence in turn", or: "One person reads until he makes a mistake, then the next person takes over." Experience has shown that while the students may well concentrate on the reading itself during these games, they do not tend to absorb the meaning of the text.

Questions

After the reading, give your young people the chance to ask questions about words or expressions in the text before you go on to the next point.

YOUCAT SESSION

The YOUCAT session works in exactly the same way as the Bible session, except that you work with the relevant question from the YOUCAT. Here again, every young person should have a copy of the YOUCAT in front of him. Read the text together, and give them an opportunity to ask questions.

DISCUSSION
Encourage open discussion

This point is intended to enable the young people to discuss and debate the relevant texts among themselves. In order to foster a genuinely open discussion, it is important that the young people should be able to express their real opinions openly. It is necessary, therefore, that you take good care to ensure that all the participants address one another with mutual respect, allowing the other person to finish what he is saying and being open to the expression of opposing views. This is true even where the opinions and ideas expressed diverge a long way from the Christian faith.

Make the Catholic Christian position quite clear

Now, however, it is important that you make absolutely clear what the position of the Catholic Church is in this matter, so as not to give the impression that the Church doesn't really know quite what she thinks, either, and that therefore any view is more or less okay.

GETTING STARTED
Marathon vs. Confirmation

Theological basis

The YOUCAT Confirmation course book compares Confirmation with a marathon and suggests a "four-step" training plan for the young people, comprising: participation in the course, Sunday Mass, regular prayer, and Bible reading. The aim is to make the young people understand that, without proper preparation, nothing will be achieved. This was something that Saint Paul had already understood.
B → **1 Cor 9:24–27**

The Confirmation candidates should be made to understand that in Confirmation they will receive "power" from above—the power of the Holy Spirit. This training program likewise has its own team of trainers, namely, the Bible, YOUCAT, and the Confirmation course book. And, of course, you. However, the Chief Coach is God himself, in person.
Y → **203**

The candidates need to be clear that this is not a matter of some kind of theory but, rather, that they themselves, as young adults, need to engage more intensively with God. They should—as the course book shows with Mother Teresa—be like power cables carrying the current of God so that light can shine on earth. The Holy Spirit, whom we receive in Confirmation as the gift of God's own self, is the power circuit that unites us with God and with one another as Church, so that we are not people who live in the dark.

A brief observation: the impulse for this sometimes also takes effect only belatedly. Your Confirmation catechesis has not therefore already failed simply because there is no immediate sign of "success". Sometimes there are still waters, where everything seems to pass over without effect. That does not, however, mean that nothing is happening within these young people with respect to the Confirmation course. On the contrary, an encounter, a brief moment, a phrase from the Bible or from the YOUCAT can remain for years in the memory. Suddenly, this memory awakens and only then begins to take effect. You should therefore also be relaxed in your Confirmation classes and not expect too much of them or of yourself. Our faith is always a matter between the individual and God himself.

Back to the text: The first lesson is an opportunity to get to know one another, and so it simply briefly outlines the "four steps"—involvement in the course, Sunday Mass, regular prayer, and Bible reading—which the young people can then reread and start to practice as a training program. These steps are also meant to help them get to know God better and start to converse directly with him themselves. If you should start to wonder whether that is not asking a little too much, then here are a few thoughts to reassure you:

Every training program begins with the first step. Marathon, running, movement ... Basically, what we mean by religion is always a way to God. It is surely the case that all the major world religions are in some way earnestly seeking something "higher", something beyond the merely human. The religious understanding is as old as mankind itself: the belief that there is more to life than this life, this here and now; that there is something that transcends this life. But does this "something" actually exist?

At all events, we already assume this "something" whenever we speak of the world as a whole or about our death. That part of us which quite naturally reaches out beyond our bare existence is what we call the human spirit. It is a spirit that for thousands of years has contemplated this "other" world. Philosophy and theology, religion and the Church, and likewise poets and artists also move in this world and are inspired and fascinated by it. Already, when two people fall in love, the world seems to open up. Similarly, the love between parents and their children and the spirit of genuine friendship lead into this world.

Thus there is something that points to this non-material world, to a world "behind the tangible", "behind physics" (or "metaphysical"). So far so good, but there is no certainty in relation to this "something". In the Christian understanding of religion as a way to God, there is another fundamental dimension that enables us to believe with all our hearts, namely, the fact that God has come to meet us of his own accord, has communicated himself to us in history, in word and deed, has finally shown himself to us, in Jesus Christ, as he really is and now accompanies us on our way in Jesus Christ.

Our way through life is a way with God, which finally ends once more in God. This way began for us with our Baptism, when our parents and godparents professed the Catholic faith on our behalf. First Holy Communion was a first solemn high point, when we received Jesus Christ in the consecrated Host. Now we are about to take the next step, which involves truly coming to know our faith so that we can also say in response to it: "Yes, this is what I believe." And so that we can convey it to others, also. This is the reason why the Holy Spirit is promised to us in Confirmation. What happens in this sacrament is a gift of God to us. Whoever truly embraces this gift will certainly pass it on to others.
Y → 197

That is the reason for the Bible (Step 4), so that we can look up everything in it ourselves. But also the reason for Holy Mass (Step 2), for here this self-giving of the Son to the Father is celebrated in such a way that it is actually made present. That's enough for now. We will go into detail about prayer (Step 3) in Chapter 8, where it is also the principal topic of the lesson.

LESSON

1

CATEGORY

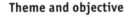

Getting Started—Here We Go

Theme and objective
Getting to know one another in the group
Introducing the young people to the idea of personal prayer

Preparation
🔥 Get the cards ready for the *Conf!activity*. Go to youcatconfirmation.com >PDF RESOURCES >Lesson 1 activity. Be sure in each case to copy the correct back page onto the cards. Additionally, you will need a standard set of dice, plus paper and pencils.

Introduction
Give your group the following game as a quick way to get to know one another: Everyone has to give his first name, a Church-related term beginning with the same letter as his name, his favorite food, and his favorite character from a movie, book, or TV show. Give your young people a short time to think about it first. For the sake of simplicity, it's best if you start first.

Basic ground rules
Next you can give some brief information about the basic rules for the Confirmation course—for example, how often and for what reasons they are allowed to miss, and what the consequences will be in each case. This would also be a good moment to explain briefly the rules about how to behave toward one another.

Conf!activity

Next thing on the program is Conf!activity. (Incidentally, we went to great lengths to give the game as goofy a name as possible—and I think we succeeded.) Divide your group into two teams, and deal the cards into three separate stacks (mime, draw, describe). The participants take turns throwing the dice. Depending on the number thrown, the player takes a card from one of the three stacks:

1 and 2 "mime it"
3 and 4 "draw it"
5 and 6 "describe it".

The other members of his team have to guess the word, while the opposing team makes sure he plays by the rules (e.g.,"Miming doesn't mean speaking or humming or singing!" and "Drawing doesn't mean writing or putting down numbers or using foreign languages!"). For every card correctly guessed, the team gets a point. Once the cards in one stack are used up, the game can continue, using the remaining cards. The winning team is the one with the most points at the end.

Conclusion and prayer

So that you can also get a little closer to God during your Confirmation course, we are inviting you to take on our prayer challenge: Take at least ten minutes each day, during this Confirmation course, to have a real conversation with God. And you will find that something happens in your relationship with God.

Lord Jesus Christ,
we are preparing to receive the sacrament of Confirmation.
Be with us and help us each day to understand better what your life and your message mean for us. Come to meet us during the weeks before us, as we try to get to know you better. And give us a helping hand whenever we get lazy and try to get out of spending time with you.
Amen.

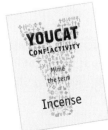

2 HE EXISTS?, HE DOESN'T EXIST? ...
What We Can Know about God

Theological basis

In the course book, the young people get to know about atheism, which in our days is particularly aggressive in its approach and simply rejects outright the idea that believers can be rational thinkers. Y → 5 And yet there are arguments for God that are so good that they have been called "proofs" of God's existence. The course book touches on one such argument, in which the so-called "cosmological proof of God" (the universe cannot have its cause within itself) and the "proof from causality" (everything that exists has a cause) come together. Take a look at www.youcatconfirmation.com to see what other "proofs" for God there are. Y → 41–45

A powerful argument is the existence of the tiny grain of sand, which raises the question of why there is anything at all rather than nothing. B → Ps 53:2

But then things really get interesting. The fact that God exists is something we can reach by the power of our own reason; but when it comes down to who God is and what he is like, then we need to be careful, for then we must stick strictly to what God tells us about himself. Y → 7

What? He speaks to us? Is it not rather the case that he remains silent? Isn't that perhaps the reason why people do not believe? Why doesn't he step in with all his power, say, in Syria, or in some other country where people are massacring one another, and tell them straight out who's who and make them stop it at once?

But if God were to show himself, to reveal himself, in such a way that all we can then do is say, "Okay, God. Whatever you say; we will obey", then his intervention would have the quality of an absolute command. If God were to intervene in me from the outside in this way, like a system administrator in my PC, and perform whatever operations he considered necessary, regardless of what I happened to be doing at the time, then he would simply be turning me into an automaton.

Could it be that this talk about the silence of God ultimately reflects the fact that we would like a God to speak with such clarity that we no longer have to decide for ourselves, no longer have to take a position, no longer have to believe, because we are completely overwhelmed by the absolute? That we want a God who would, so to speak, flatten us? Then he could sort out all the other things at the same time, clean everything up properly, couldn't he?

Whether it be the longing for God to speak to me directly or the longing to be merged completely with him in love or the longing for his ordering rule, his justice—all these things are profoundly human yearnings that also have their place and their value in theology and in the teaching of the Church. But there is only one such longing that God will not fulfill—and that is to take away our freedom from us. For this does not correspond with God's plan. He has created us to be free. We are the ones who must accept his revelation. We ourselves are the ones who must work and strive to be united with him. And we are likewise the ones who have to act; we have to do good, while knowing that it will remain the work of man. And yet—to avoid a further error—God does not leave us all alone in this. Without his help, we can neither recognize his revelation nor believe in him nor act as he intends.

Essentially, God's revelation begins with his creation. It bears testimony to God; its order, beauty, and complexity point beyond itself—to God. Y → 4

Man is created "in the image of God". For us he is a God with a Name. B → Ex 3

"God is love" B → 1 Jn 4:16. A love that has been revealed in Jesus Christ. Y → 56

So now we are already deep in the Bible text. But what makes this text the word of God? How do we know that this is God's revelation? We do not have the kind of knowledge here that we can normally take for granted—for example, that Washington, D.C. is the capital of the United States of America. But if someone tells me that his father has died, then I can generally assume that it is true. In fact, I would even tell other people that I know it. I know it from his son. This is the critical point: Can we trust the witnesses? That is not an issue that requires much reflection—for witnesses appear in court, and, on the basis of the testimony of these witnesses, judgments are made, legal verdicts issued. The credibility of a witness can determine whether another person is sent to jail.

But who are the witnesses in regard to the Bible? First and foremost, those who actually wrote it. Thus Saint John writes in his first Letter: "That which was from the beginning, which we have heard, which we have seen with our eyes, which we have looked upon and touched with our hands, concerning the word of life" (**B → 1 Jn 1:1**). This is someone who is at pains to ensure that he relates the experiences he himself has had, in other words, things he has seen, heard, and touched.

The Gospels do not contradict anything we know from history. Indeed, many details are confirmed by sources outside the Bible. And there are four evangelists and other authors of the New Testament who essentially confirm the same events concerning Jesus. (Secular history is in many cases much less solidly supported, and yet few people cast doubt on it.) Many of these early Christians traveled long distances and endured great hardships in order to tell of these happenings and spread their faith. They were imprisoned, tortured, and killed. Thus they sealed by the witness of their lives what they had written and recounted. Who would be willing to die for an invented story?

We have already spoken about how both the natural world and man himself bear witness to God. At the beginning of the Bible, man is described as being made in the image of God. As the reality of God, Jesus Christ finally concludes this revelation. (We will see how the understanding of this revelation later unfolds still further with the Church.) Through Jesus, God has definitively stated: "See, this is who I am." **Y → 10**

That is why we believe in him, as someone who has lived among us. Our faith relates to an event—the Christ Event. It is the relationship to a Person, to the Person of Jesus Christ. And not merely to a book ...

LESSON

2

CATEGORY

What We Can Know about God

Theme and objective:
Three aspects: God has created us out of love; he wants to make contact with us; and he wants to spend eternity together with us.

Preparation

- Photocopy the illustrations about our ideas of God from the materials supplied and make eight cards out of them. You can of course make several copies of the individual pictures, so that everyone can take part in the same exercise. Illustrations found on pp. 17–20.
- Photocopy each of the pictures: on the creation of man, the burning thorn bush, and Jesus (pp. 21–23).
- Photocopy scripture verses on pp. 24–25. (All worksheets are available at youcatconfirmation .com.)

Introduction
Lay out the copies with the different representations of God, and ask your group members to pick out the one that corresponds most closely to their own ideas. When everyone has chosen, go around the group asking them to give the reasons for their decision.

Link
You can lead on to the next point by saying something like this: "Now that we have all thought a little about our own ideas of God, let's take a look at what God himself has to say about it. God has given us a few indications of what he is like, and I imagine you've already heard some of them."

God as Creator

Place the picture of Adam and Eve in paradise in the center, and get one of your young people to tell you the story. If there is no one in your group willing to do so (as experience has shown, young Confirmation candidates can vary widely), tell the story yourself or read the verses from the Bible: **B → Gen 1:26–31** Ask the group what this Bible text tells us about God and his relationship to man.

For the present topic, the following aspects are important:

- God finds that man is good (**B → Gen 1:31**).
- God has created man without seeking to harness him for a particular purpose (but purely out of an abundance of overflowing love—see also **Y → 59**).

God reveals himself to man

Proceed in exactly the same way with the image of Moses and the burning thorn bush (cf. **B → Ex 3:1–6,13–14**). What is important is to make clear to your students that God, on his side, wants to make contact with man.

God reveals himself in Jesus Christ

Now take the picture of Jesus and his disciples, and encourage them to tell what they know about Jesus. What is above all important for our topic is that God reveals himself to us in Jesus, in other words, we see in Jesus what God is like. You can also point them to **B → Jn 14:9** ("He who has seen me has seen the Father").

Link

Lead on to the next point by saying, "We've heard what God reveals to us about himself. Now let's take a look at how he actually sees us."

Who am I to God?

Look now with your group at two key passages from the Bible that quite clearly characterize God's relationship to us:

"No longer do I call you servants, for the servant does not know what his master is doing; but I have called you friends, for all that I have heard from my Father I have made known to you." (**B → Jn 15:15**)

"For God so loved the world that he gave his only-begotten Son, that whoever believes in him should not perish but have eternal life." (**B → Jn 3:16**)

You can either read the two passages from Saint John's Gospel directly from the Bible with your group or else lay out the two cards with the verses on them, so that everyone can read the text.

DISCUSSION

Discuss with your candidates what the two passages say about God's relationship to us. What is important is that he sees us as his friends (**B → Jn 15:15**) and that he sends his Son to save us (**B → Jn 3:16**). You can also point out to your group that in the last-mentioned verse we could even substitute the words "the world" with "you".

Link

You can lead in to the conclusion of the lesson by saying something like this: "We will now finish by taking a look at the plan that God has in mind for us."

What does God want for me?

Together with your young people, read the answer in bold type to YOUCAT Question 1, or simply place the corresponding card in the middle. Explain to them that God's plan for us is that we all live one day with him in heaven. This is God's plan for us, because he loves us infinitely. (You can also illustrate this plan with the quotation from **B → Jn 17:24**.)

DISCUSSION

After a brief discussion about God's plan, end the hour with a prayer.

Conclusion and prayer

Dear God,

You have created us all out of love. You want to be close to us and to live with us. Help us in our everyday lives actually to behave like friends of yours, and at the end of our lives, take us into your eternal company.

Amen.

LESSON

2

CATEGORY

What We Can Know about God

Theme and objective:

Three aspects: God has created us out of love; he wants to make contact with us; and he wants to spend eternity together with us.

Bonus approach

For this topic we have thought of an additional approach that you could possibly use, either instead of the methods described below or even in addition to them, beforehand.

In the video *The Footprints of God: Moses*, Steve Ray depicts Moses' encounter with God. Show your group a clip of *The Footprints of God: Moses* video (available online at www.ignatius.com).

Then you can ask your students if the portrayal of God in this video matches their own idea of him. Share your own ideas of God with one another.

Preparation

Photocopy the illustrations, showing the different representations of God, from the material provided and make eight cards out of them. You can of course make more than one copy of the individual pictures, so that more people can choose the same representation. Photocopy the bible passages on pp. 24–25 or download at youcat confirmation.com.

Introduction

Lay out the copies with the different representations of God, and ask your group members to pick out the one that corresponds most closely to their own idea of him. When everyone has chosen, go around the group again, asking them to give the reasons for their decision.

Link

You can lead on to the next point by saying something like this: "Now that we have all thought a little about our own ideas of God, let's take a look at what God himself has to say about it."

Bible group work

Divide your students into three groups. Each group is given one of the three texts and allowed roughly ten minutes time to answer this question: "What does the Bible passage tell us about God and about his relationship to us?"
You can either photocopy the corresponding Bible passages or have your students read them directly from the Bible.

Group 1: **B** → **Gen 1:26–31** (the creation of man)
Group 2: **B** → **Ex 3:1–6,13–14** (God reveals himself to Moses in the burning thorn bush)
Group 3: **B** → **Jn 14:8–11** (God reveals himself in Jesus Christ)

Presentation of the results

The three groups will now present their findings. They should do so in the right chronological order (creation, Moses, Jesus).

In the presentation and in any ensuing discussion, the following aspects should be highlighted:
- 🔥 God finds that man is good (B → **Gen 1:31**).
- 🔥 God has created man without seeking to harness him for a particular purpose (but purely out of an abundance of overflowing love—see also Y → **2**).
- 🔥 God makes contact with man (B → **Ex 4:14**).
- 🔥 God reveals himself in Jesus Christ (B → **Jn 14:9**).

Link
Lead on to the next point by saying, "We have heard what God reveals to us about himself. Now let us take a look at how he actually sees us."

BIBLE SESSION "WHO AM I TO GOD?"
Read together B → **Jn 15:15**: "No longer do I call you servants, for the servant does not know what his master is doing; but I have called you friends, for all that I have heard from my Father I have made known to you."
What is important here is that God sees us as his friends.

Then read B → **Jn 3:16** "For God so loved the world that he gave his only-begotten Son, that whoever believes in him should not perish but have eternal life." In discussing this passage afterward, you can point out that at this point we could equally replace "the world" with the word "you". In this way, you can make still clearer just how immensely important every single one of us is in God's eyes.

Link
You can lead on to the final topic of the lesson by saying something like: "Now that we have seen how important we are to God, we need to ask ourselves what plan God actually has in mind for us."

BIBLE SESSION "WHAT DOES GOD WANT FOR ME?"
Read together B → **Jn 17:24** ("Father, I desire that they also, whom you have given me, may be with me where I am, to behold my glory which you have given me in your love for me before the foundation of the world"). Explain to your group that what is meant here is that God wishes to have communion (be united) with us in eternity.

YOUCAT SESSION "WHAT DOES GOD WANT FOR ME?"
Read Y → **1** ("For what purpose are we here on earth?"), and share your ideas about it with the group.

Conclusion and prayer
Gracious God,
You have created us all out of love. You want to be close to us and to live together with us. Help us also, so that in our ordinary lives we can really behave like your friends, and, at the end of our lives, take us up into your everlasting community.
Amen.

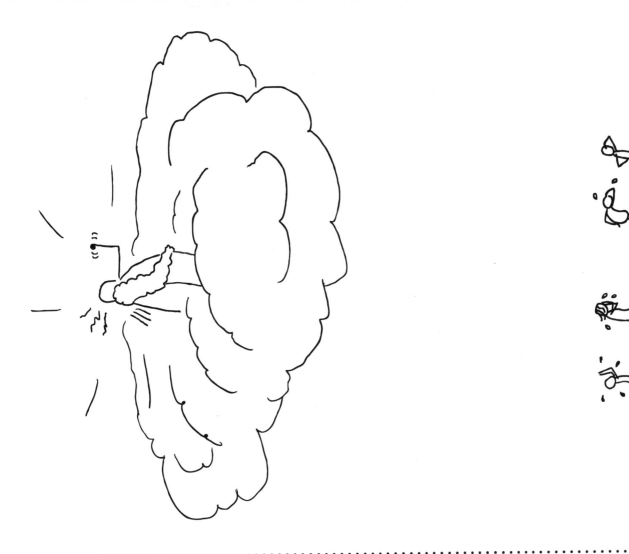

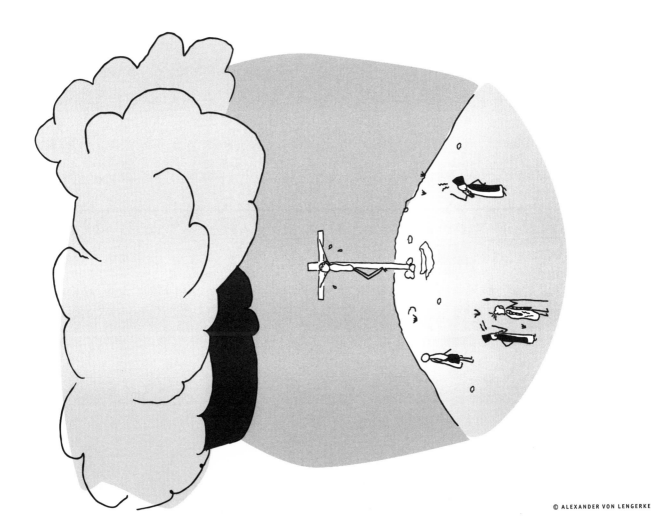

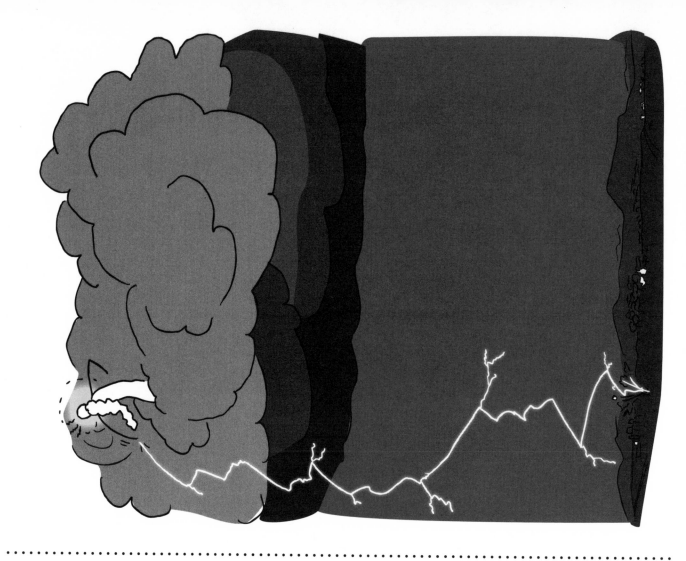

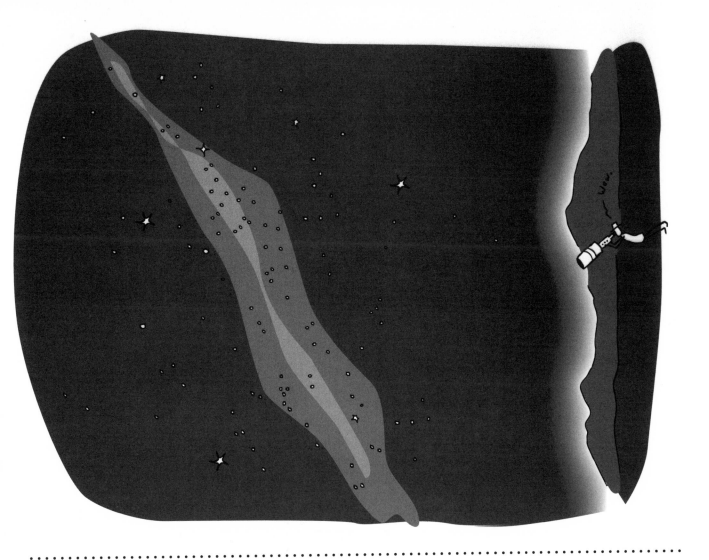

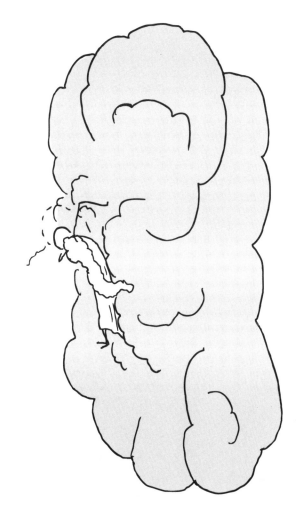

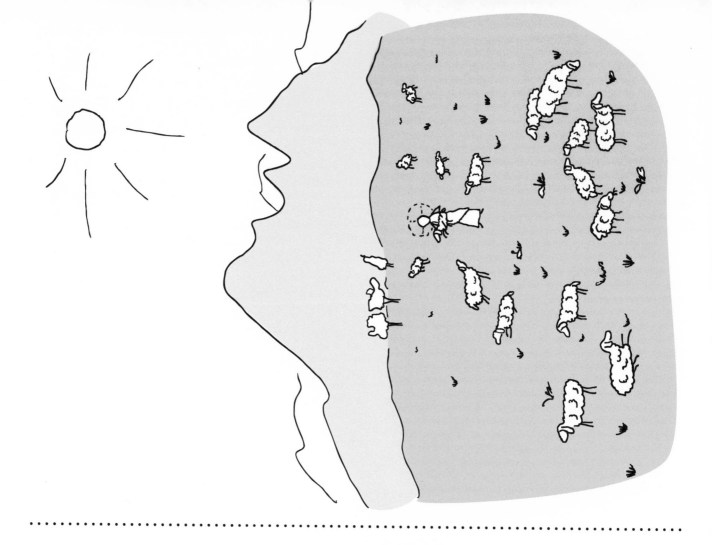

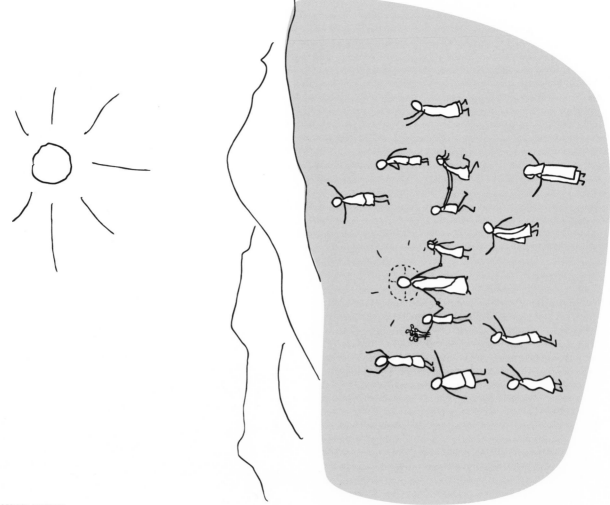

"No longer do I call you servants, for the servant does not know what his master is doing; but I have called you friends, for all that I have heard from my Father I have made known to you."

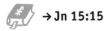 → Jn 15:15

"For God so loved the world that he gave his only-begotten Son, that whoever believes in him should not perish but have eternal life."

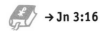 → Jn 3:16

"We are here on earth in order to know and to love God, to do good according to his will, and to go someday to heaven."

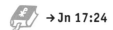 → 1

Jesus says: "Father, I desire that they also, whom you have given me, may be with me where I am, to behold my glory which you have given me in your love for me before the foundation of the world."

→ Jn 17:24

Theological basis

The notion of an idyllic, unspoiled "natural" state of man is somewhat naive. Saint Paul was a good deal more realistic about this, for he noticed that he again and again ended up doing exactly the opposite of what he had recognized as good and right. B → Rom 7:15–25

Sometimes, when we struggle with things like eating and exercise, we are inclined to blame our "weaker selves". Sometimes this weaker self can gain the upper hand within us, and then we end up committing "little sins" (venial sins). But this same pattern of giving way to our weaker selves can also apply to situations that are much more serious than things like eating too much chocolate and watching too much TV and being "couch potatoes", because it springs from a fundamental imbalance within us. For the good and evil tendencies are not actually equally present within us but, rather, our nature is conscious of a clear tendency toward evil. Our "weaker self" so often seems to be the stronger!

Not only you and I, but every single person, without exception, suffers from this inner defect that makes us tend toward sin. This tendency toward sin is in fact the wound we have inherited from original sin. Y → 68–70

This tendency is not the same as personal sin, therefore, but is rather an inclination toward sin, a weakening of our will and understanding. And this is something we all share, from the day of our birth. Where this comes from is described in the Bible by the story of the Fall. It is the story of how evil came into the world, and hence it is the answer to an ancient question.

If we look briefly at the story of the Fall (B → Gen 2:7–15, Gen 3) we are struck, for example, by:

- the fact that the name Adam means "man" and Eve means "life". "In him all men have sinned", says Saint Paul. We are all Adam;
- the fact that the serpent promises: "You will be like God" (B → Gen 3:5);
- the nature of Adam's sin. It is a transgression, born of curiosity and greed; a transgression springing from covetousness.

From the beginning, we owe everything to God. He it was who created us and placed us in a paradise. We could have gone on living like this, in a spirit of gratitude and trust, but we have allowed ourselves to be deceived into mistrusting him and rejecting his will. We have allowed ourselves to be seduced into wanting to be dependent on him no longer but, instead, to be ourselves like God ("You will be like God, knowing good and evil"). We imagine ourselves to be masters over life and death (abortion, euthanasia, war, murder), and we even want to play the creator ourselves (gene manipulation, nanotechnology, cloning).

Avarice is the mother of all evils. While man was still living, carefree and in harmony, in a garden that he tended, something (the serpent) seduced him into thinking that was not enough. Now even God himself, to whom he owed everything, became an object of reproach because he was keeping something back from him, begrudging him something. Simply because not everything was possible, simply because there was a limit ...

And what does that have to do with us? In Baptism, we were washed clean of the inborn stain of original sin. But still within us, along with our strength as creatures of God, there remains a basic attitude of desire. With the love of God, we can use this desire for a good end, but because of it we are also inclined to give way to temptation and to sin. This is the unbalanced state within us, our fallen nature, the thing we call our "weaker self". But it is no good saying, "That's the way I am. That is my nature!" We are still responsible for our own individual actions, for, although our nature is weakened, our freedom has not been taken away.

CATEGORY

COGNITIVE

Why the world is broken

Theme and objective:
Original sin and personal sin
Man separated from God. The first sin (original sin) destroyed the harmony between God and his creation and continues to affect us to this day.

Preparation
- Get a few fairly recent newspapers and magazines as well as a pair of scissors for each of your students.
- Photocopy the cartoon (on p. 32) "Sin destroys our bond with God." (Also available at youcat confirmation.com)

Introduction
Get your students to look up examples of evil in the world in the newspapers and magazines. Then go around the group, asking them to present their findings and also to say a few words themselves about the events. Point out to them at the same time that while there are some things for which individuals are directly responsible, because they hurt other people, or risk hurting them, in other cases nobody seems to be directly responsible.

DISCUSSION
Ask your group members whether they think the world is mainly good or mainly bad.

NB: Some of the students in your group may perhaps express the view that evil is necessary so that we can recognize the good or at least give it its true value. Without evil, there is no good, either, they say. You can probably counter this dualist error at the outset by suggesting that you can really enjoy a big ice cream sundae even if you have not eaten something really disgusting beforehand. Behind this argument is the entirely valid experience that even good things can lose their attraction when we get too much of them. But the real problem is the lack of variety and not the absence of evil. In a world without evil, things would by no means be boring or monotonous. Such a danger exists only in a world with no variety. But this is not what God has planned for us.

Link
You can lead on to the next point by saying something like, "Now let's look at the answer Christianity gives to the question of how evil really came into the world—a world that God actually planned and created to be very good."

BIBLE SESSION ON THE FALL
Read together the account of the Fall (B → Gen 2:16–17, 3:1–13,17–19, 23–24).

Input
Explain to your students that the story of Adam and Eve and the serpent uses imagery to tell us how evil came into the world. For example, this figurative language depicts God in very human terms, in the way he walks through the garden and Adam and Eve even hear his footsteps. The serpent stands for personified evil, which attempts to estrange man from God.

Guided Bible discussion
Now go through the text with your young people with the help of the questions below. Since the account of the Fall is really challenging, you will often have to supplement the discussion with the additional information we have printed beneath the questions by way of explanation.

What trick does the serpent use to persuade Eve to eat the fruit? (B → Gen 3:1)
The serpent deliberately misrepresents God's commandment (B → Gen 2:16–17) in order to sow mistrust. Eve at first resists the attempt, but she then makes God's commandment sound stricter than it really is (B → Gen 3:3).

What promises does the serpent make? (B → Gen 3:4–5)
When the serpent talks about "knowing good and evil", this does not mean the simple ability to distinguish between good and bad deeds—something man is already capable of doing through his conscience—but knowledge in a more

comprehensive sense, rather like the omniscience of God. That is why the serpent also promises that man will become like God. In this way he provokes the desire within man to determine for himself what is good and evil—and in so doing to separate himself from God. It is here that the real sin lies.

Why does Eve decide to eat the forbidden fruit? (B → Gen 3:6)

Eve allows herself to be blinded by these empty promises; she sees only the supposed advantages of the forbidden fruit and then tries to justify her decision to herself, although she knows full well that her decision was wrong. The dialogue between Eve and the serpent mirrors the inner conflict in our own consciences when we waver between the seduction of sin and the voice of God. The sense of mistrust that the serpent so successfully fosters here—whether God really has our best interests at heart with his commandments—can then often lead us to decide against God.

What consequence does the breaking of this commandment have on the relationship between God and man? (B → Gen 3:7–8,23–24)

The deliberate rejection of God's will separates man from God. This is made clear in the text when Adam and Eve suddenly feel ashamed and hide away from God. The original harmony between God and man has been destroyed by the decision of man. The "expulsion from paradise" is described in the Bible text as the punishment that God imposes on man. However, in reality, it is also the necessary consequence of man's own decision to set himself against God and thereby destroy the harmonious relationship with God (i.e., paradise).

What consequence does the breaking of the commandment have on the relationship of men with one another? (B → Gen 3:12–13,16)

This sin also destroys the harmony in the relationship between men. This is made clear in the text when Adam and Eve feel ashamed in front of each other and make themselves clothes out of fig leaves. But this disharmony between men has other bitter fruits as well: for example, Adam and Eve both try to blame someone else. Eve blames the serpent for her own decision, while Adam blames Eve and even attempts to blame God himself. This now damaged relationship between men still characterizes our behavior toward each other today. This is not the way it was planned by God but is the consequence of the Fall.

What are the consequences of the Fall for the whole of creation? (B → Gen 3:17–19)

Through this, the very first sin in world history, not only is the relationship broken between God and man and between one man and another, but the whole of creation is deprived of its original harmony. This is made clear in the text when God speaks of the ground having been cursed because of Adam's sin. In the life of paradise, man never went hungry but had every kind of fruit to eat; but now he has to feed himself painfully and with hard labor. All in all, creation has been broken. From now on, suffering and death will be a part of life. Hence, for man, the world is no longer in the state of perfection in which God created it but is damaged by sin. It is not completely destroyed, and man can still recognize the hand of God, for example, in its beauty, but now it carries within itself the tendency toward evil. Here again, it is important to understand that man has caused this himself by his own decision to sin. The destruction of this harmony is not God's will (even if the figurative language of the Old Testament appears to suggest that here) but is the consequence of man's own actions.

NB: Your Confirmation candidates might well come up with the quite reasonable question of why God put a forbidden tree in the middle of the garden in the first place and so actually led man into temptation. Here again, of course, the text is using figurative language. It is a matter here of the freedom that God has given man. For in order to be able truly to love God, man must be free. Otherwise, it would not be love. But true freedom also implicitly involves the possibility of making a disastrously wrong decision, thereby destroying even freedom itself. The tree in the middle of the garden is an image of this dilemma of freedom.

YOUCAT SESSION

Read Y → 68 together ("Original sin? What does the Fall of Adam and Eve have to do with us?"), and exchange your thoughts about it.

Input: Sin

Take up the idea again that it is man who separates himself from God through sin (and not the other way around, because God is angry, for instance, or offended), and explain it with the help of the cartoon (p. 32) showing man destroying his relationship with God. Just as original sin did, so too every sin we consciously commit separates us once again from God. In this way, man destroys his relationship with God, separates himself from God. This gulf, created by man, is one that man can no longer overcome by his own strength (see also Y → **162**).

Looking ahead

Explain to your students that, despite the separation from God, caused by us men, God still continues to seek communion with us. In order to overcome the gulf we have created, he has sent us his own Son to free us from sin. Just how God's plan has worked in practice is what we will be talking about in the next two lessons.

Conclusion and prayer

Father in heaven,
may I give honor to your name!
May your rule dawn, and may you alone be King,
just as you are in heaven, so too in my soul and in the whole world.
Help me to recognize, to love, and to do your will:
May your will be done on earth and in my life.
Help me to be contented with the bread that you give
and to share gratefully with others.
Help me to forgive others and not bear a grudge;
for I know that you love them and are merciful to them,
just as you also forgive me and help me to make a new start.
And when temptation oppresses me, then stand by me;
send me your Spirit and strengthen my will,
so that through your strength I can resist evil.
And grant peace in our days.
Come to help us with your mercy
and preserve us from confusion and sin,
so that we can await, with full confidence,
the coming of our Redeemer Jesus Christ.
With you alone is the kingdom and the power and the glory
in eternity.
Amen.

Why the world is broken

Theme and objective:

Original sin and personal sin

Man separated from God. The first sin (original sin) destroyed the harmony between God and his creation and continues to affect us to this day.

Preparation

◉ Get a few fairly recent newspapers and magazines as well as a pair of scissors for each of your students.

◉ Photocopy the cartoon (on p. 32) "Sin destroys our bond with God."

Introduction

Get your students to look up examples of evil in the world in the newspapers and magazines. Then go around the group, asking them to present their findings and also say a few words themselves about the events. Point out to them at the same time that while there are some things for which individuals are directly responsible, because they hurt other people, or risk hurting them, in other cases nobody seems to be directly responsible.

DISCUSSION

Ask your group members whether they think the world is mainly good or mainly bad.

NB: Some of the students in your group may perhaps express the view that evil is necessary so that we can recognize the good or at least give it its true value. Without evil, there is no good, either, they say. You can probably counter this dualist error at the outset by suggesting that you can really enjoy a big ice cream sundae even if you have not eaten something really disgusting beforehand. Behind this argument is the entirely valid experience that even good things can lose their attraction when we get too much of them. But the real problem is the lack of variety and not the absence of evil. In a world without evil, things would by no means be boring or monotonous. Such a danger exists only in a world with no variety. But this is not what God has planned for us.

Link

You can lead on to the next point by saying something like, "Now let's look at the answer Christianity gives to the question of how evil really came into the world—a world that God actually planned and created to be very good."

Short skit about the Fall

Divide your students into two groups. Give them approximately fifteen minutes to prepare a largely improvised play, using as their basis **B → Gen 2:15–17 and 3:1–13.**

Give the first group the task of reenacting the way in which the serpent (the devil) sets out to persuade Eve to eat from the Tree of Knowledge. The performance can of course be improvised and go beyond the Bible text, but it must correctly portray the direction of the argument.

The second group prepares to reenact the way in which God, Adam, and Eve react after the Fall. Here again, what matters above all is that the play accurately portrays the essence of the biblical account.

DISCUSSION

Following the presentation of these two short plays—and the well-earned praise for those performing them—discuss together what became particularly clear to your students in preparing, performing, or watching the performances.

In the discussion, the following aspects should emerge clearly (if necessary, coming from you):

◉ When the serpent talks here about "knowing good and evil", he does not simply mean the ability to distinguish between good and bad deeds—something man is already capable of doing through his conscience—rather, he means knowing in a more comprehensive sense, similar to the omniscience of God. That is why the serpent also promises that man will become like God. In this way he provokes the desire within man to determine for himself what is good and evil and in this way to separate himself from God. It is here that the real sin lies.

- The dialogue between Eve and the serpent mirrors the inner conflict in our own consciences when we waver between the seduction of sin and the voice of God. The sense of mistrust that the serpent so successfully fosters here—whether God really has our best interests at heart with his commandments—can then often lead us to decide against God.

- The consequence of sin is separation from God. However, it is man who, through his own decision to sin, actively separates himself from God and through his own action creates the rift between himself and God. Moreover, by his own efforts he can no longer overcome this gulf that he himself has created.

- Sin also leads to disharmony among men. Adam and Eve both try to blame someone else. Eve blames the serpent for her own decision, while Adam blames Eve and even attempts to blame God ("The woman whom you gave to be with me": **B → Gen 3:12**).

NB: Your Confirmation candidates might well come up with the quite reasonable question of why God put a forbidden tree in the middle of the garden in the first place and so actually led man into temptation. Here again, of course, the text is using figurative language. It is a matter here of the freedom that God has given us. For in order to be able truly to love God, we must be free. Otherwise, it would not be love. But true freedom also implicitly involves the possibility of making a disastrously wrong decision, thereby destroying even freedom itself. The tree in the middle of the garden is an image of this dilemma of freedom.

Input: Sin
Take up the idea again that it is man who separates himself from God through sin (and not the other way around: because God is angry, for instance, or offended), and explain it with the help of the cartoon (p. 32) showing man destroying his relationship with God.
Originally there is a harmonious communion between man and God.
Through sin, man destroys this relationship, however, and separates himself from God. This gulf, created by man, is one that man can no longer overcome by his own strength (see also **Y → 162**).

YOUCAT Session
Read YOUCAT **Y → 68** together ("Original sin? What does the Fall of Adam and Eve have to do with us?"), and exchange your thoughts about it.

Input—consequences of original sin
Explain to your young people that not only has the decision by Adam and Eve to oppose God's will led to the fact that all men now have a "broken" relationship with God, since they have inherited this mistrust toward God along with original sin, but, in addition, this very first sin has damaged the whole of creation. Hence the world is no longer in the state of perfection in which God created it but is damaged by sin. It is not completely destroyed, and man can still recognize the hand of God, for example, in its beauty, but now it carries within itself the tendency toward evil.

Looking ahead
Explain to your students that, despite the separation from him, caused by us men, God still continues to seek communion with us. In order to overcome the gulf we have created, he has sent us his own Son to free us from sin. Just how God's plan has worked in practice is what we will be talking about in the next two lessons.

Conclusion and prayer
Father in heaven ... (see p. 29).

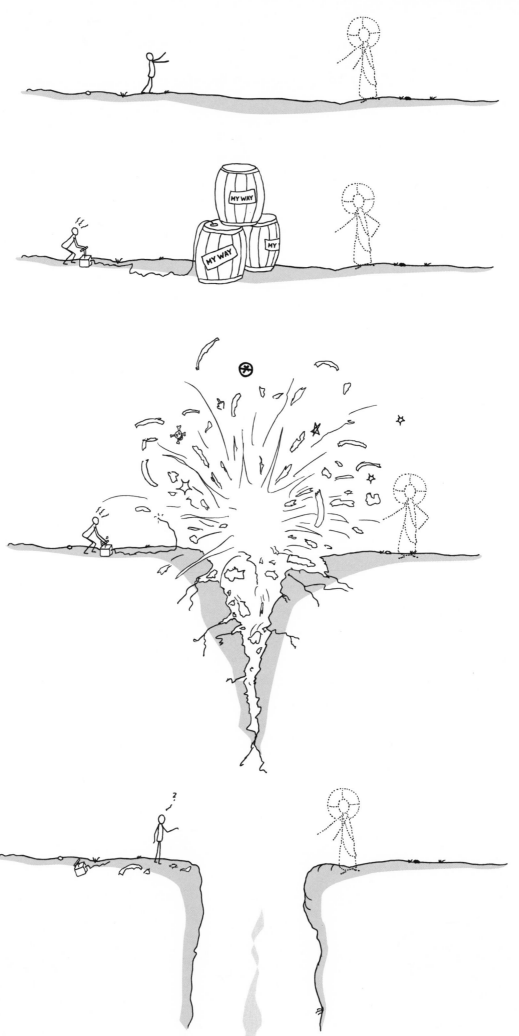

Jesus—More than a Mere Man

Theological basis

Many people still claim, even today, that this Jesus of Nazareth never existed. When people say this, you need to ask first if they really mean that a historical figure so well-documented by Christian and non-Christian evidence in the ancient world never actually existed—in which case you can perhaps help overcome such blatant ignorance with a little literary research. Or do they perhaps mean that Jesus was quite different from the person we know him to be—in other words, having nothing to do with God's Son or the Resurrection and so on—but was simply a wandering Jewish preacher who lives on today only in his teachings, etc. ... No doubt you've heard that one before as well. The fact that people are hardly likely to let themselves be locked up, tortured, and executed for believing in some crazy guru is a fairly solid counterargument, but then unbelief can be very stubborn at times.

So there's Jesus and God—and then there's pure mythology, which was all quite normal in the Hellenistic culture of the time. The gods would have sex with women—or the goddesses with men—and beget children, who would then be "demigods", like Hercules, for example. But Jesus was no demigod. He was true God and true man (Y → 77), fully God and fully man. Through Jesus Christ, the invisible God becomes visible. He becomes man like you and me. Y → 9

And so faith in Jesus Christ, the Son of God, is not quite so incomprehensible as some people like to think.

The other variant of the argument, which held sway through most of the fourth and fifth centuries and which is becoming very popular again today, goes something like this: "Jesus Christ was a man, but with a special relationship to God." But that simply ignores what Jesus is and what he has told us.

Jesus himself revealed to us what we know about the Trinitarian God. He is the *Son* who speaks of his *Father in heaven*. B → Jn 10:30

He prays to the Father to send us the Holy Spirit and instructs us to baptize in the name of the Trinitarian God, the Father, Son, and Holy Spirit. B → Mt 28:19

We believe in one God in three Persons. We do not pray to three different gods; we pray to one single Being who shows himself to be triune and yet remains One. Y → 35

This mystery of God's being is by no means self-explanatory and is somewhat tricky to understand. Of course one can always ask why it is that God is three Persons. The answer is: Because already, within his own being, he is One who loves. The relationship of the three Divine Persons to one another is love. God is Love. This is the mystery that Jesus Christ has revealed to us. Y → 36

And because God is love, he has come to us in Jesus Christ, has become man; he has reached out to his beloved creatures and become one of them. Y → 76

Jesus was no guru, keeping a group of paying supporters, with whom he maintains a distant relationship in order not to undermine his leading role, his status. He did not sit, unapproachable, on a throne, accepting homage and tribute. No, Jesus showed his feelings and met people at their own level. Y → 79

- Jesus has friends and weeps (at the raising of Lazarus): B → Jn 11:17–44
- Jesus withdraws into solitude, prays, experiences anguish: B → Mt 26:36–46 (Mount of Olives, Y → 100)
- Jesus weeps: B → Lk 19:41
- Jesus sleeps: B → Mt 8:24
- Jesus seeks to withdraw with his disciples and rest awhile: B → Mk 6:31

- Jesus becomes angry (when he casts the money-changers out of the Temple): B → Jn 2:15–17
- Jesus is tempted by Satan: B → Mt 4:1–11, Y → 88
- Jesus can sympathize with our weaknesses: B → 4:4–16

He was a man of flesh and blood, a man people could see and touch. Yet in the first Bible passage mentioned above, the raising of Lazarus, he also shows that he is Lord over life and death. He does something that God alone can do. He raises a dead man back to life. Not a man feigning death; not someone whose heart or breathing has temporarily stopped and who has been revived after a quarter of an hour or so. No. Lazarus has been dead for four days. Jesus prays to the Father and then calls Lazarus to come out.

This episode shows how, on the one hand, Jesus behaves like an ordinary man, moved to tears at the death of a friend, yet how, on the other hand, Jesus, through his entirely intimate relationship with the Father (i.e., of God with God, within the divine nature), builds a bridge from our human frailty, mortality, and even death—which is the mark of fallen man—to eternal, immortal, true life (which has no end); in other words, to God himself. That is why, in one Church hymn, we sing, "Mystery of faith—in death is life." It is a mystery that finds its fullest expression at Easter, when Jesus himself rises from the dead.

This bridge, which the God-man Jesus builds, from man to God, from death to life, has the classic mediator function—Christ the priest, as mediator between man and God. The remarkable thing about this mediator is, first of all, the fact that he is no other-worldly medium, no enraptured guru or unapproachable cult-leader, but a loving, sympathetic man who has experienced all the same temptations that we have; who knows our weaknesses and loves us nonetheless. And there is another remarkable thing about this mediator—he has no need to make himself important, to make a big noise, put on a show. For he is already God. He shows the loving face of God to us.

LESSON

4

CATEGORY

Who is Jesus?

Theme and objective:
Jesus is true man and true God.
Jesus knows exactly what it is like to be human, because he himself has become man.

Preparation
- Get a roulette wheel with the alphabet on it and also all the letters of the alphabet from a Scrabble game (or else make them yourselves out of cardboard).
- Photocopy the Jesus puzzle (p. 40), and stick it onto a piece of stiff cardboard, then cut out the individual parts of the puzzle. If you have a fairly large group, it is probably a good idea to enlarge the puzzle with a photocopier (also available at youcatconfirmation.com).

Introduction
Have each of your students spin the roulette wheel in turn or draw a letter from the Scrabble tiles or cutout cardboard squares. Each person must immediately and spontaneously call out a word or phrase that has something to do with Jesus and that begins with this letter.

If the connection with Jesus is not obvious, by all means ask the pupil to explain why he has chosen this word. If any of the participants come up with entirely inappropriate phrases, don't hesitate to step in at once and say this is not allowed.

Linking to the lesson theme
Let the youngsters play a few rounds, and then call a halt to the game, saying something like "You've come up with a few expressions that (more or less) have some connection with Jesus. We're now going to look at one or two aspects that are important in regard to Jesus."

Jesus Puzzle—Man or God?

Divide your students into two groups and get them to listen to the Bible readings below on the life of Jesus. One group must listen for everything that points to the fact that Jesus is a man. The other group should listen for everything that points to the fact that Jesus is God.

In the center of the group, lay out the first three pieces of the puzzle below (with the words "Jesus", "Man", and "God") so that everyone can see them.

Now read aloud the following New Testament passages (or relate them in your own words) in the order given below:

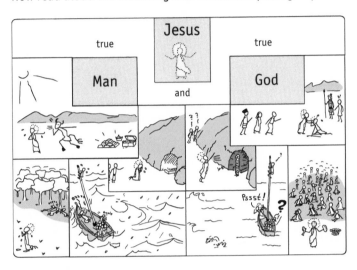

B → Mt 4:1–11—After fasting in the desert, Jesus is hungry and is tempted by the devil.
B → Mk 10:46–52—The healing of the blind beggar, Bartimaeus.
B → Lk 22:39–45—Jesus suffers fear and anguish on the Mount of Olives and prays to his Father.
B → Lk 9:12–17—The multiplication of the loaves.
B → Mk 4:35–41—The storm on the Sea of Galilee. Jesus sleeps, then silences the storm when the disciples wake him.
B → Jn 11:17–19,34–41,43–44—Jesus grieves over Lazarus and then raises him from the dead.

After each reading, get the group to respond.

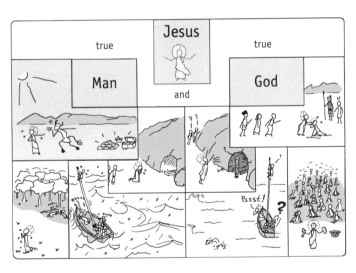

After reading about the temptation of Jesus, place the puzzle piece showing *hunger and temptation* on the human side. Your pupils might rightly argue here that Jesus resisted the temptation (which is theologically extremely important!), but essentially this is still something a man would be capable of doing. In fact, we are all called to resist the temptations of the evil one.

The *healing of the blind man* shows the divine power that Jesus possesses. Place this piece of the puzzle on the "divine" side.

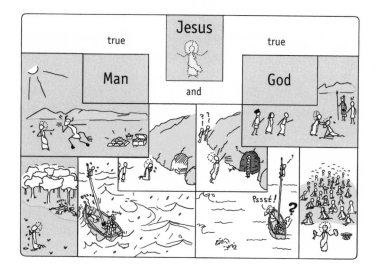

The *fear and anguish of Jesus* clearly show his human side. This piece of the puzzle belongs on the "human" side.

The *multiplication of the loaves* clearly shows his divine power, so of course it belongs on the "divine" side.

The account of the *storm at sea* allows us to see both the divine and the human side of Jesus. His sleeping through the storm could be seen as showing his serenely trusting human side, while his power over the elements clearly shows his divinity. Put one of these two mirror-image puzzle pieces on each side.

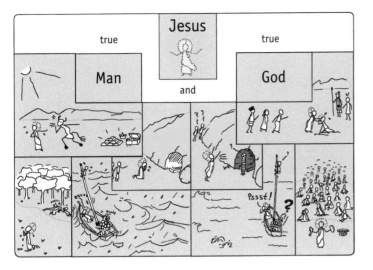

In the *raising of Lazarus*, Jesus clearly shows his power over death—in other words, his evident divinity. At the same time, however, his sadness at the death of Lazarus also shows his human side. Put the two tiles in their respective places on either side.

DISCUSSION
Now give your students a short while to discuss what has emerged so far. You can get the discussion started by asking if, in their opinion, Jesus was man, then, or God.

Input
Now place the final piece of the puzzle: *true—and—true* in place. Explain to your pupils that Jesus was fully God and fully man—in other words, not a mixture of the two (a "demigod"). You can introduce this by reading question **Y → 77** in YOUCAT.

Input
Read the following passage from **B → Heb 4:15**: together with the candidates: *"For we have not a high priest who is unable to sympathize with our weaknesses, but one who in every respect has been tempted as we are, yet without sinning."*

Short group work session
Divide your students into small groups and give them five to ten minutes to think about the following questions:
- What advantage is it to us if the person who intercedes for us before God knows what it is like to be human, with all our human feelings and with the experience of having faced temptation?
- What advantage is it to us if our mediator before God is himself also God?

Discussion on the results from the group work
Get each group to present their ideas. What should emerge clearly from these ideas or from the ensuing discussion is the fact that Jesus, as true man, is in a position really to understand our problems and feelings, because he himself has experienced them also. That even applies to the situations in which we have been tempted and have sinned, because he too has been tempted (though without ever sinning: **Y → 88**).

Conclusion and prayer
Lord Jesus Christ,
you became man, and you yourself know everything we have to go through in our lives. You know what it feels like to be human, and you know what it feels like to be tempted. Support us in our lives, and help us whenever we are tempted to go in the wrong direction.
Amen.

Who is Jesus?

Theme and objective:
Jesus is true man and true God.
Jesus knows exactly what it is like to be human, because he himself has become man.

Preparation

👐 Get a roulette wheel with the alphabet on it and also all the letters of the alphabet from a Scrabble game (or else make them yourselves out of cardboard).

👐 Photocopy the worksheet (p. 41 or youcatconfirmation.com) for each of your students and remember to provide pencils, too.

Introduction

Have each of your students in turn spin the roulette wheel or draw a letter from the Scrabble tiles or cutout cardboard squares. Each person must immediately and spontaneously call out a word or phrase that has something to do with Jesus and that begins with this letter.

If the connection with Jesus is not obvious, by all means ask the pupil to explain why he has chosen this word. If any of the participants come up with entirely inappropriate phrases, don't hesitate to step in at once and say this is not allowed.

Linking to the lesson theme

Let the youngsters play a few rounds, and then call a halt to the game, saying something like "You've come up with a few expressions that (more or less) have some connection with Jesus. We're now going to look at some of the more important aspects in regard to Jesus. And so we're going straight to the most important written source we have about Jesus, namely, the Bible."

BIBLE SESSION
B → Jn 11:17–19,34–41,43–44

Together read the text of Saint John's Gospel—ideally chapter 11, verses 17 to 19 and then from verse 34 to 44. You might also leave out verse 42, since it could perhaps cause confusion.

Worksheet

Give each of the Confirmation candidates a copy of the worksheet "Jesus brings Lazarus back from the dead", and ask them to work on it quietly for the next ten minutes. If need be, point out that this is not a test or a quiz. Instead, the students should choose answers that really reflect what they think.

DISCUSSION

The questionnaire is meant to serve as a starting point for a discussion that should make both the humanity and the divinity of Jesus particularly clear. The emotions shown by Jesus in the scenes depicted, and of course particularly the way that Jesus weeps for his friend Lazarus, make it clear that he is truly human, while in the raising of Lazarus he shows he is God.

Get your students to read their answers in turn. Normally, this should lead to a discussion on the Bible text itself. If little discussion is forthcoming, however, then you should go straight on to your summary. If your young people are inclined to dwell on the less relevant aspects, then lead the conversation back to the central aspects, without, however, forcing a discussion of these aspects. If necessary, bring the discussion to a conclusion by saying something like: "In addition to the aspects you have raised, it seems to me that there are two very important things in the text", and then go straight on to the summary.

Summary

You can sum up the discussion like this: "In the Bible passages we have just read together, two things emerge very clearly about Jesus—the first is that he is both true man and true God. His humanity is shown in the way that he grieves over Lazarus and even weeps. Yet at the same time he is God, as we see above all in his power to raise Lazarus from the dead. But that doesn't mean that Jesus is half God and half man or some kind of demigod; rather, he is both true man and true God at the same time, as the theologians put it. Let's turn now to YOUCAT to see exactly what is meant by that."

YOUCAT SESSION

Read question Y → 77 in YOUCAT together. Then you can perhaps go on to Y → 100 as well, in order to complete the picture.

DISCUSSION

Discuss the YOUCAT text together, and consider how we are to understand the fact that Jesus is indeed "true God and true man".
If the discussion does not give rise to the question of why this should be so important or what difference it makes to us, you can put the question to them yourself at the end of the discussion: *What does it mean for us, as Christians, that Jesus is both true man and true God?*"

BIBLE SESSION
B → Heb 4:14–16

Read the Bible text together. Explain that in the old Jewish Law, the high priest is understood to be a mediator between God and man.

DISCUSSION

You can use the following questions to prompt a discussion:
- What advantage is it to us if the person who intercedes for us before God knows what it is like to be human, with all our human feelings and with the experience of having faced temptation?
- What advantage is it to us if our mediator before God is himself also God?

It should emerge clearly from the discussion that Jesus, as true man, is in a position really to understand our problems and feelings, because he himself has experienced them also. This even applies to situations in which we have been tempted and have sinned, because he too has been tempted (though without ever sinning: Y → 88).

Conclusion and prayer

Lord Jesus Christ,
You became man, and you yourself know everything we have to go through in our lives. You know what it feels like to be human, and you know what it feels like to be tempted. Support us in our lives, and help us whenever we are tempted to go in the wrong direction.
Amen.

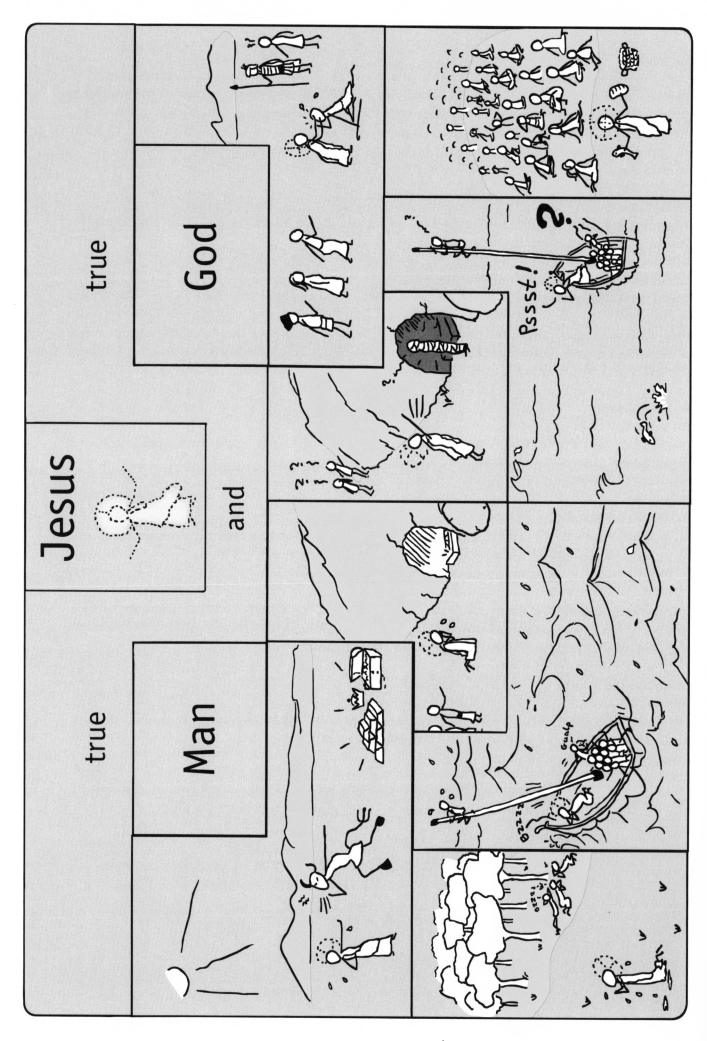

Jesus brings Lazarus back from the dead

Jn 11:17–19, 34–41, 43–44

1. What surprised you most in the account of the raising of Lazarus?

☐ That Jesus was able to raise the dead.
☐ That Jesus wept because Lazarus had died.
☐ That Lazarus had been buried in a cave.
☐ That Jesus had not prevented Lazarus from dying.
☐ That anyone really believes this story.
☐ ☐ ☐

2. What do you think this account tells us about Jesus?

☐ Jesus is a weakling, because he cries in public.
☐ Jesus is a powerful magician who can wake the dead.
☐ Jesus is God.
☐ Jesus is true man and true God.
☐ ☐ ☐

3. What do you find most important about the story of Lazarus?

☐ That Jesus is a man, who has feelings and can be sad.
☐ That Jesus is God and can raise the dead.
☐ That Jesus is a man and has friends.
☐ That Jesus is God and that we can still be friends with him.
☐ The story means nothing to me.
☐ ☐ ☐

4. Who do you think Jesus is?

☐ An invented figure, a bit like Harry Potter.
☐ A wise teacher who lived 2000 years ago and had some good ideas.
☐ A prophet, who spoke God's message and showed us how we ought to live.
☐ The Son of God.
☐ ☐ ☐

Theological basis

Jesus, of all people—in whom we see human goodness incarnate—was executed, was put to death in the most brutal possible manner. Why? And it seems that he was fully aware of what was going to happen, yet still freely submitted to this suffering. Again, why? **Y → 96, 97**

The difficulties in understanding the relationship between God and man in Jesus Christ, which we saw in the preceding chapter, were exactly the same as those faced by his own contemporaries. Was it God who was working powerfully in Jesus? Or was the Nazarene a conman—and a blasphemer? In Jewish Law, that was punishable by death. Jesus was convicted and put to death by the Roman occupying power, using the most cruel and humiliating punishment of his day. **Y → 101**

Caution: the question of who exactly was to blame for the crucifixion and death of Jesus could backfire, since in fact we have all of us crucified him and continue to crucify him to this day—through our sins of hatred, cynicism, laziness, cowardice, lying, and betrayal.

In the previous chapter, it was made clear that God does not stand idly by while man slowly destroys himself and the world around him through the chain reaction of sin. So what does he do exactly? He sends us Jesus Christ, as Savior and Redeemer, to snatch us from the power of evil. **Y → 70**

The one who was to rescue us had to be more than merely human, as we are, since it is we who created an unbridgeable gulf of sin between ourselves and God. On the one hand, he would have to be truly human, not some kind of half-and-half being and not an angel. For he had to represent mankind, which had turned away from God. And so the man who would make this change of direction had to be somebody who was "like us in all things but sin"—a sinless person, totally faithful to God and totally trusting in God. He would have to be as obedient as Abraham was, who was prepared even to sacrifice his own son.

The prophet Isaiah described just such a person in his famous "Songs of the suffering Servant" (**B → Is 42:1–9, 49:1–9, 50:4–9, 52:13–53:12**). This man would bring light and justice to all nations. But in return, he himself would have to suffer outrage and humiliation on behalf of mankind—even to the point of sacrificing his own life. And yet, "he shall prolong his days" (chap. 53). Isaiah's prophecy of the suffering servant, who suffers and atones for others, is nothing less than a prophecy of the coming of the "Christ", the "Messiah"—both words mean the "anointed one". This is exactly what the risen Jesus himself explained to his disciples on the road to Emmaus (**B → Lk 24:25–27**) and what they in turn reported to the others (see **B → Acts 8:30–35**).

And so God himself, in Jesus Christ, the incarnate Son of God, takes on the full consequences of man's separation from God. And since God is Love, separation from God ultimately implies hatred and violence. And because man's turning away from God, the Creator, who created us in love, can only be deeply painful to him (some theologians speak of "insulting" God), the path of redemption can only be a path of suffering. Hence Jesus takes all this suffering upon himself. All this power of godlessness is bundled together, concentrated, and focused in what we have called the "killer punch" that was aimed at Jesus Christ, the God who revealed himself in the form of man. At the end of it all, this "God as man" is dead. Yet he himself has fulfilled the sacrifice of Abraham. **Y → 73**

This is no accident—and neither is it a tragic disaster. Jesus was "delivered up according to the definite plan and foreknowledge of God" (**B → Acts 2:23**). He himself also knew this: "... For this purpose I have come to this hour" (**B → Jn 12:27**). One of the real steps forward in our understanding of our faith is this realization that all of this was the consequence and expression of God's love. Father and Son were inseparable allies in this mission, willing, and even filled with longing, to take on this ultimate suffering out of love for mankind and to carry this love all the way through to the Cross, against all the evil of the world—and willing, even from the Cross, to bestow loving forgiveness. It is Love, on both sides, that has proved itself in the extremity of the Cross. Y → 98

Pope Benedict wrote a moving meditation on the way in which Jesus united his will with the will of his Father in the Garden of Gethsemane, on the Mount of Olives, on the night before he suffered:

" 'Not my will, but your will be done.' What is this will of mine, what is this will of yours of which the Lord speaks? My will is 'that he should not die', that he be spared this cup of suffering: it is the human will, human nature, and Christ felt, with the whole awareness of his being, life, the abyss of death, the terror of nothingness, the threat of suffering. Moreover, he was even more acutely aware of the abyss of evil than are we who have a natural aversion to death, a natural fear of death. Together with death, he felt the whole of mankind's suffering. He felt that this was the cup he was obliged to drink, that he himself had to drink in order to accept the evil of the world, all that is terrible, the aversion to God, the whole weight of sin. And we can understand that before this reality, the cruelty of which he fully perceived, Jesus, with his human soul, was terrified: my will would be not to drink the cup, but my will is subordinate to your will, to the will of God, to the will of the Father, which is also the true will of the Son. And thus in this prayer Jesus transformed his natural repugnance, his aversion to the cup and to his mission to die for us; he transformed his own natural will into God's will, into a 'yes' to God's will."

And now let us look back at the human tendency, the tendency of all of us, to oppose the will of God. What does Jesus do through his freely accepted suffering, in which he takes upon himself the sins of all mankind, he whom we are meant to imitate? *"Jesus draws our will—which opposes God's will, which seeks autonomy—upward, toward God's will. This is the drama of our redemption, that Jesus should uplift our will, our total aversion to God's will, and our aversion to death and sin and unite it with the Father's will: 'Not my will but yours'. In this transformation of 'no' into 'yes', in this insertion of the creaturely will into the will of the Father, he transforms mankind and redeems us. And he invites us to be part of his movement: to emerge from our 'no' and to enter into the 'yes' of the Son. My will exists, but the will of the Father is crucial because it is truth and love"* (April 20, 2011).

Easter is the time when we celebrate this redemption through Jesus Christ. The feast of Easter is also known as the "three holy days", or, in Latin, the *Triduum Paschale*. On the previous Sunday, Palm Sunday, Jesus entered Jerusalem. Holy Week then begins, and on the Thursday of this week the Church commemorates the Last Supper, the institution of the Eucharist. After this, and after Jesus' prayer and agony on the Mount of Olives, in the Garden of Gethsemane, he is arrested. This is the beginning of his Passion. Good Friday is the day of the crucifixion and, hence, a day of fasting and abstinence. Holy Saturday is the day when Jesus rests in the tomb. On Easter Sunday we celebrate the Resurrection.

The sequence of these days also illustrates our redemption. Through his Passion and death on the Cross, Jesus Christ has taken the sins of the entire world upon himself. He has entered into death and has done so entirely as man, not merely as an immortal God to whom it can make no difference. With this we come to a truly black moment in salvation history, the moment when God dies. We recall that death is a consequence of original sin, the ultimate consequence of our estrangement from God; that at the end of each human life the individual either returns to God or turns away from God, in a final and definitive No, into death. This is the state of "godforsakenness" of which Jesus speaks on the Cross, shortly before his death. In Jesus Christ, God, so to speak, enters into the denial of himself. This "realm of death" is what the Jews called *Sheol* and the Greeks, *Hades*. As we say in the Creed: "He descended into hell." This is Holy Saturday.

LESSON

5

Why Did Jesus Have to Die?

CATEGORY

🔥 🔥 🔥

EMOTIONAL

Theme and objective:
Jesus dies for us on the Cross.
Jesus has suffered for us; we can respond by living our lives with him.

Preparation

- Get the following objects or a picture of them: three nails, a hammer, a crown of thorns, a scourge. You could also perhaps make drawings or representations of them yourself.
- Look for a film portal on the Internet that has a clip of the short Czech film *Most* (*The Bridge*) (between five and seven minutes duration, depending on the version).

Introduction

Lay out some of the so-called "instruments of the Passion" (in other words, the things that remind us of the sufferings of Jesus) in front of your group. Wait, first of all, to see how your students react. Then, with the help of the individual items, you can talk to them about the sufferings Jesus endured. It may perhaps be necessary to emphasize that Jesus really did suffer (because he really was fully human).

If you feel it appropriate for your group, you can even hammer a large nail into a wooden beam, in order to illustrate what the crucifixion meant.

Link

"We have just seen that Jesus really did suffer greatly from his crucifixion. Now we need to ask the question why Jesus actually allowed that to happen to him."

If need be, you can remind them at this point that Jesus definitely had the opportunity to run away or hide. So, humanly speaking, his execution was not inevitable.

BIBLE SESSION

Read the following Bible passages with your group:
B → Lk 22:7,14–15,19–20 (the Last Supper) and
B → Jn 13:1,3–10,12–15; 15:12–13

DISCUSSION

Now discuss together what reasons the Gospel texts give for the fact that Jesus took the agony of the crucifixion upon himself.

The following aspects should emerge from the discussion (if your students don't come up with them, you can raise them yourself):

- "This is my body which is given for you", and again "This chalice which is poured out for you is the new covenant in my blood." So Jesus is giving his life for his disciples (and hence for us as well). And in doing so, he also institutes the Eucharist.
- By washing his disciples' feet—which was a task normally done only by menial servants—Jesus makes it clear that the reason for his actions is simply love.
- "Greater love has no man than this, that a man lay down his life for his friends." Here Jesus tells us once again quite plainly that love for his disciples and for us is the reason why he takes upon himself the suffering of the Cross.
- He also urges his disciples—and us, too—to love just as he has loved.

YOUCAT SESSION

Read together YOUCAT Y → 101 "Why did Jesus have to redeem us on the Cross, of all places?"

Link
You can lead on to the next point by saying something like this: "If God has truly suffered and truly died for us, then he cannot be some kind of remote, impersonal God, sitting far away somewhere on a cloud, with no idea about our lives. So he has truly come close to us. And yet the death of Jesus has a still deeper meaning."

Input: Sin separates us from God
Use the cartoon on p. 32 to remind your group of the problem: namely, that man has cut himself off from God through sin and cannot overcome this separation by his own efforts. (See the lesson on sin.) Now God has to deal with the following problem: he wants to (re-)establish friendship with man (see the discussion of God's plan for us, pp. 14–15), but man is no longer capable of coming back to him. For the gulf, the abyss that he has created through his sin, is simply still there—just as the bad things we have done are still there (as a historical fact) and cannot simply be washed away from the timeline, even if we do regret them.

God's solution
Since our guilt cannot simply disappear, there is only one solution: someone else has to take it on for us. And it has to be someone who hasn't any sin on his own shoulders. And so God decides to take matters into his own hands. God (and by that we mean the second Divine Person, the Son) becomes man in Jesus Christ and, by his death on the Cross, takes all our guilt upon himself. Now, thanks to his sacrifice, we are once more able to approach God.
To illustrate how Jesus has restored our way back to the Father, you can show them the cartoon "The Cross—Bridge over the Abyss" (see p. 48).

In place of others
Generally speaking, it is rather difficult, of course, to understand the concept that Jesus took on our guilt. To explain this, you could, however, point out that even in the ordinary human sphere it is possible for someone to sacrifice himself for others. Some of the examples best known to your students would undoubtedly be from films, such as *Gran Torino* or *Titanic*. But there are still more impressive examples—of people who truly have given, or at least risked, their lives for others. People such as Saint Maximilian Kolbe, who volunteered his life for a fellow prisoner and died in his place.

DISCUSSION
At this point, it is perhaps a good moment to engage in a discussion about God's plan of salvation for us and to clear up any questions the group may have, since this is quite a difficult subject. After this you can continue with an explanation of our part in this plan.

Input: Our part in God's plan of salvation
Jesus has opened up the way to God, so that we can once again approach him. However, he cannot force us into friendship with God, since love that is forced is not love at all. And so our task is to respond to this unique offer from God by deciding for him, deciding to love him just as he has loved us. This means, therefore, that we allow him into our lives and try to live according to his will. The first step in this direction was taken by our parents when we were baptized, when God freed us from original sin. But now it's our turn to decide—to turn freely toward him and to keep returning again and again when we have made a mess of things. So, to use the same image: Jesus has cleared the way for us; now it is our job to walk toward God.

Film *Most* (*The Bridge*)
You can finish by showing your group the half-hour film *Most* (*The Bridge*). Actually, it might be more sensible to shorten the film to a single clip (about five minutes). The film is about a drawbridge operator whose son sacrifices himself in order to save a train full of people. It is a quite moving illustration of what Jesus has done for us, and, at the same time, by showing the suffering of the father, it clears away the false cliché of God the Father being cruel to sacrifice his Son for us. (You should review the film to determine beforehand its age-appropriateness for your group.)

Conclusion and prayer
You could complete this lesson with the passage from the letter of Saint Paul to the Philippians that describes what God has done for us and that is sometimes described as a hymn (B → **Phil 2:6–11**).

Have this mind among yourselves, which was in Christ Jesus, who, though he was in the form of God, did not count equality with God a thing to be grasped, but emptied himself, taking the form of a servant, being born in the likeness of men. And being found in human form he humbled himself and became obedient unto death, even death on a cross. Therefore God has highly exalted him and bestowed on him the name which is above every name, that at the name of Jesus every knee should bow, in heaven and on earth and under the earth, and every tongue confess that Jesus Christ is Lord, to the glory of God the Father.

CATEGORY

🔥 🔥 🔥

COGNITIVE

Why Did Jesus Have to Die?

Theme and objective:
Jesus dies for us on the Cross.
Jesus has suffered for us; we can respond by living our lives with him.

Preparation
🔥 Get six one-quart juice cartons. Remember some plastic cups as well, if you intend to drink the juice afterward.
🔥 Photocopy the cartoons on pp. 32 and 48 (or youcatconfirmation.com).

Introduction
Divide your students into two groups, and have them build a bridge between two juice cartons that is strong enough to take the weight of a third carton. Tell them to make the gap between the two cartons wide enough so they can't simply lay one of the Confirmation books or some other book across the gap.
If you have enough space available, you could have your group build a bridge between two chairs, strong enough to support your own weight. If you do this, then you will not need the juice cartons, of course.

Input: Sin separates us from God
Use the cartoon on p. 32 to remind your group of the problem: namely, that man has cut himself off from God through sin and can no longer overcome this separation by his own efforts. (See the lesson on sin.) Now God has to deal with the following problem: he wants to (re-)establish friendship with man (see the discussion of God's plan for us, pp. 14–15), but man is no longer capable of coming back to him. For the gulf, the abyss that he has created through his sin, is simply still there—just as the bad things we have done are still there (as a historical fact) and cannot simply be washed away from the timeline, even if we do regret them.

God's Solution
Since our guilt cannot simply disappear, there is only one solution: someone else has to take it on for us. And it has to be someone who hasn't any sin on his own shoulders. And so God decides to take matters into his own hands. God (and by that we mean the second Divine Person, the Son) becomes man in Jesus Christ and, by his death on the Cross, takes all our guilt upon himself. Now, thanks to his sacrifice, we are once more able to approach God.
To illustrate how Jesus has restored our way back to the Father, you can show them the cartoon "The Cross—Bridge over the Abyss" (see p. 48).

In place of others
Generally speaking, it is rather difficult, of course, to understand the concept that Jesus took on our guilt. To explain this, you could, however, point out that even in the ordinary human sphere it is possible for someone to sacrifice himself for others. Some of the examples best known to your students would undoubtedly be from films, such as *Gran Torino* or *Titanic*. But there are still more impressive examples—of people who truly have given, or at least risked, their lives for others. People such as Saint Maximilian Kolbe, who volunteered his life for a fellow prisoner and died in his place.

DISCUSSION

At this point, it is perhaps a good moment to engage in a discussion about God's plan of salvation for us and to clear up any questions the group may have, since this is quite a difficult subject. On the other hand, depending on how receptive your group is, you could also present this discussion after the Bible session.

BIBLE SESSION

Divide your students into two groups. Give each of the groups one of the two Bible passages and the task to read it with your comments in mind and afterward to present it to the entire group.

Group 1: B → 1 Pet 2:24–25

In this passage Saint Peter explains that Jesus himself has taken the blame for us ("... bore our sins") by his death ("his wounds"). When he speaks of the "Shepherd and Guardian of your souls", he means Jesus, of course.

Group 2: B → Rom 3:23–26

In this passage Saint Paul also declares that Jesus has taken our sins upon himself ("as an expiation") by his death ("by his blood"). What is new about this passage is that Saint Paul emphasizes that we have been saved without having deserved to be. This means that God has freely saved us (i.e., out of love) and not because we have done anything to deserve it ourselves.

Input: Our part in God's plan of salvation

Jesus has opened up the way to God, so that we can once again approach him. However, he cannot force us into friendship with God, since love that is forced is not love at all. And so our task is to respond to this unique offer from God by deciding for him, deciding to love him just as he has loved us. This means, therefore, that we allow him into our lives and try to live according to his will. The first step in this direction was taken by our parents when we were baptized, when God freed us from original sin. But now it's our turn to decide—to turn freely toward him and to keep returning again and again when we have made a mess of things. So, to use the same image: Jesus has cleared the way for us; now it is our job to walk toward God.

Link

Take the phrase "justified by his grace as a gift" (B → Rom 3:24) and at the same time the passage (B → Rom 3:28) "For we hold that a man is justified by faith apart from works of law", and ask your students if anyone can earn heaven by good or pious works. Let them briefly suggest answers to this question.

Input

Explain to your group that it is indeed impossible to earn salvation or achieve it by good works alone. We can only accept God's free gift of forgiveness. In other words, we cannot purchase our place with God or do so many good works that we have a right to it. And so when we try to live in the spirit of Jesus, this is our grateful reaction to the redemption that God has already granted us as a free gift and not in return for something we have done.

However, because we have been created to be free, we still have the capacity to destroy our newly given gift of communion with God, again and again, through sin. But fortunately we can come back again to God just as often, through the Cross of Christ (more on this in the lesson on confession).

Conclusion and prayer

You can complete this lesson with the passage from the letter of Saint Paul to the Philippians that describes what God has done for us and that is sometimes described as a hymn (B → Phil 2:6–11).

Have this mind among yourselves, which was in Christ Jesus, who, though he was in the form of God, did not count equality with God a thing to be grasped, but emptied himself, taking the form of a servant, being born in the likeness of men. And being found in human form he humbled himself and became obedient unto death, even death on a cross. Therefore God has highly exalted him and bestowed on him the name which is above every name, that at the name of Jesus every knee should bow, in heaven and on earth and under the earth, and every tongue confess that Jesus Christ is Lord, to the glory of God the Father.

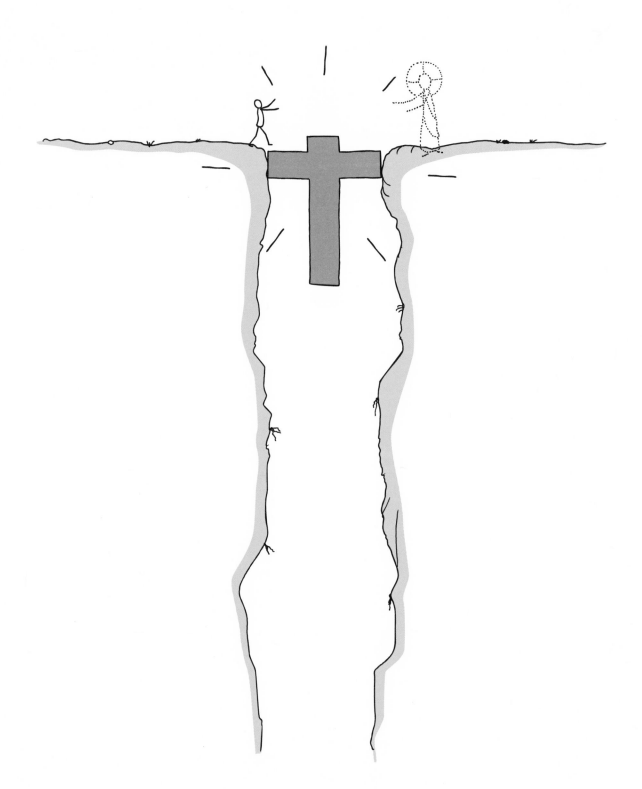

THE COMEBACK OF JESUS ... OR

The Story of the Resurrection

Theological basis

All in all, the prospects look bad for beginning a world religion when its founder dies right at the beginning. The fact that Jesus was truly dead is beyond doubt. Had he survived his crucifixion, then surely his supporters would have gone around proclaiming this story, hailing Jesus as a hero, rather than inventing this odd story of a resurrection. Y → 103

So he was dead, then. And to think that his followers had put so many hopes in him! Just how crushed the disciples must have been after the crucifixion is made clear by the story of the road to Emmaus. But it also makes clear that the disciples did not have the least idea who Jesus really was and what had actually happened. B → Lk 24:21

What is particularly important about this account is that the disciples recognize that it is the Lord Jesus himself who has been walking with them only when he actually breaks bread—and so repeats exactly what he had instituted on the evening before his Passion, in the room of the Last Supper. So, right from the start, the "breaking of bread" is the characteristic sign of the Christian assembly on the "Lord's day", or Sunday, the day on which Jesus rose from the dead. B → Acts 2:42

So the Resurrection—despite the messianic prophecies in the Scriptures (our Old Testament) and despite what Jesus himself had prophesied—was something utterly unexpected, and yet in retrospect, so to speak, it was at the same time the most plausible explanation, if we are to understand what happened afterward. Y → 105

One thing that is crucial to our faith in the Resurrection is the credibility of the witnesses, and consequently we need to give special attention to the signs pointing to their genuineness. The Resurrection of Jesus from the dead was first proclaimed by appealing to the testimony of people who were still alive at that time. This is true even if we accept the latest possible suggestions for the dating of the New Testament writings. And as to the notion that his body was "stolen from the tomb", this much at least can be said: it would not have worked. Besides, in the key witness statements for the Resurrection—the Gospels—the most important witnesses come off very badly, for at the very least they had crumbled like cowards, if they did not actually deny Jesus. And with Mary Magdalen, as a woman, there is one witness to the Resurrection who in those days would not even have been allowed to testify in court—because she was a woman. Y → 106

Jesus appears, in his glorified body, in the midst of his disciples, who, for fear of suffering the same fate as he did, have barricaded themselves in the upper room of the Last Supper. He breathes on them with his Spirit (B → Jn 20:22–23) and confers on them the authority to forgive sins and to retain sins—something that involves much more than merely the sacrament of Penance. For at a deeper level, it means here belonging to the Church. The disciples are being told to enlarge the circle of the closest friends of Jesus and to carry his message out into the whole world.

With the Resurrection of Jesus on Easter Sunday begins the triumphal march of the gospel into the whole world. One after the other, the apostles start moving, and, within the space of about thirty years, they have reached all the cultural centers of the age, and from there they powerfully proclaim the gospel of Jesus Christ, the risen and living God. Y → 108

The fact that Jesus Christ is living and is also present wherever his disciples witness to him with authority and celebrate his mysteries is made especially clear in the conversion of Saint Paul. On his way to Damascus to persecute the Christians, he is thrown from his horse and hears a voice saying: "Saul, Saul, why do you persecute me?" Note here that Jesus identifies himself with his disciples, with his Church: "As you did it to one of the least of these my brethren, you did it to me." So Saul becomes Paul and the most zealous of missionaries. He establishes numerous Christian communities and writes letters about the faith that are so full of meaning that they are read out at the second reading in almost every Holy Mass. B → Acts 9

In addition to these letters, which are some of the oldest writings in the New Testament, there are the Gospels, of course. They arose from the need of the Church, in a given locality, to give a reliable account about Jesus and his message. It should be noted here that the Church is older than the Gospels.

Now we need to address the question of whether we, too, believe in Jesus as one who is risen, living, and truly present in his Church.

LESSON 6

The Comeback of Jesus—the Resurrection

CATEGORY

Theme and objective:
The Resurrection of Jesus is a fact, not a symbol.
We, too, will rise again, after death, to eternal life.

Preparation
Buy your students some chocolate Easter eggs.

Introduction
Give out your chocolate eggs to the group, and explain to them that today is going to be a sort of Easter Day in the Confirmation class.

Group work—the empty tomb
Divide your students into four groups. Each group is given a text from Saint John's Gospel and a task to go with it. Ask your young people to read through the complete text and not simply guess an answer by using the keywords.

Group 1: B → Jn 19:31–42
Examine the text for indications that Jesus really was dead.
The Roman soldiers wanted to hurry up the death of the three crucified men so that they could be taken down in time for the Sabbath. Breaking the men's legs made it impossible for them to support their weight with their feet, and so they died quickly. But when the soldiers came to Jesus, they found it wasn't necessary, because he was already dead. But to make quite sure, they stabbed him through the heart with a spear. The blood and water that poured out were a sure sign that he was already dead.
Besides this, the text mentions two other eyewitnesses, Joseph of Arimathea and Nicodemus, who themselves took down the body of Christ and laid it in the tomb.

Group 2: B → Jn 20:1–2,11–18
How did Mary Magdalen recognize that Jesus had risen? What was the significance of the empty tomb here?
The empty tomb alone did not convince Mary Magdalen that Jesus had risen. She thought at first that someone had taken the body away. It was only through her personal encounter with Jesus that she realized he had truly risen.

Group 3: B → Jn 20:1–2,11–18
Jewish society at the time of Jesus generally regarded the testimony of women as untrustworthy. What does this signify in regard to the Resurrection?
Interestingly enough, this fact is precisely an indication that the reports were true. For if Saint John had merely invented the whole story, for example, then he would undoubtedly have come up with a more credible witness than a grieving woman.

Group 4: B → Jn 20:24–28

What indications can you find in the text about whether Jesus had "really" risen or whether he had done so only in a symbolic sense?

The fact that Jesus rose again in his physical body and did not just live on through his ideas is made clear by the fact that Jesus invites the apostle Thomas actually to touch him. Jesus is so clearly physically present that Thomas can even touch his wounded hands and the wound in his side. Yet, at the same time, the fact that Jesus can enter the room in the first place, even though the disciples have locked all the doors, is an indication that Jesus now has a risen—glorified—body.

DISCUSSION

First of all, get all four groups to study their Bible text and then to offer answers to the questions. After each presentation, give your students an opportunity to ask their own questions.

YOUCAT SESSION

Together read YOUCAT Y → 106 ("Are there proofs for the Resurrection of Jesus?"), and discuss these ideas.

Link

"We have now gone into considerable detail about the Resurrection of Jesus. Some people might ask: Why is the Resurrection so terribly important to you Christians, then? The apostle Paul has dealt precisely with this point in his First Letter to the Corinthians."

BIBLE SESSION

Together read B → 1 Cor 15:12–22, and discuss the arguments Paul puts forward. You could also use a shortened version of the same text (B → 1 Cor 15:12–13,17–20).

There are two points here that are important to Paul. For one thing, the Resurrection shows that Jesus truly was God's Son. And only then can his death on the Cross redeem us also from our guilt ("if Christ has not been raised, ... you are still in your sins"). For another thing, if Jesus is still in the tomb, then there can be no resurrection for us, either, and no eternal life.

Discussion on eternal life

Ask your students what they imagine eternal life to be like. And then go on to the YOUCAT session.

YOUCAT SESSION

Together read YOUCAT Y → 153 and 154.

The important thing here is that even in eternal life we will still have a body, because we are men made up of body and soul and, hence, can perceive the entire world around us only through our physical bodies. Without our resurrected bodies, there would be something missing for us in eternal life.

Quite possibly the objection will be raised again here that it would be extremely boring in heaven if there were nothing but good things there. But here again it is true to say that the assumption that it would be boring in heaven has to do, not with the absence of evil, but with an imagined lack of variety. But we can in fact be absolutely certain that God will make sure that things are never boring in eternal life. That is why Jesus himself speaks of eternal life as a wedding feast—so you could think of it as "one big party"!

Conclusion and prayer

O God,

who by Thy only begotten Son hast overcome death, and opened for us the way to eternal life, vouchsafe, we beseech Thee, so to confirm us by Thy grace, that we may in all things walk after the manner of those who have been redeemed from their sins,

through the same Jesus Christ our Lord.

Amen.

JOHN HENRY NEWMAN

In Search of the Holy Spirit

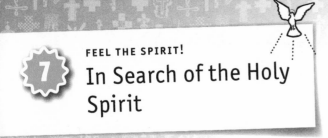

Theological basis

"Then it must have been the Holy Spirit ..." used to be what many an exasperated mother would say when none of her children was willing to admit having gotten into mischief. It's an expression that in some ways illustrates the sheer mystery, the void that the Holy Spirit represents in the life of many Christians. He is somehow incomprehensible.

This is also partly due to the images with which we have grown up: God the Father with a flowing white beard, Creator of the world, looking down from a cloud; God the Son—by far the most common theme of classical art; God the Holy Spirit—a dove. Great. The Holy Spirit is simply more abstract: Of course—because he is the relationship between the other two! Y → 38

Yet God the Holy Spirit is not just the relationship between God the Father and God the Son; for he also unites us with God and unites us human beings with one another—in love. Without him, there would be no faith. And so the Holy Spirit is extremely important to us. Y → 113–115

The meaning and purpose of being a Christian is being taken up into the love of God, into the inner-Trinitarian love, the love of the Blessed Trinity. Since the Holy Spirit is this love, being filled with him means being taken up into the love of God. This is not something that we can let happen to us, in a flash, for example by simply going to Confirmation and letting it all happen to us. The third Person of the Trinity helps us to keep on becoming better, helps us to draw closer and closer to God instead of turning away from him. Y → 118

This is not the place to write a history of the Holy Spirit. But you will doubtless recall that even in the creation account we are told that he hovered over the waters (B → **Gen 1:2**). Here one can already picture the wind, the roaring sound with which he later came over the disciples at Pentecost (B → **Acts 2:2**). But he is also there, breathing life into the first man—the "breath of life"—which in Hebrew also means the soul (B → **Gen 2:7**). And when Jesus breathes his last breath on the Cross, we are told that he "gave up his spirit" (B → **Jn 19:30**). Finally (B → **Jn 20:22**), the risen Jesus breathes on his disciples and tells them "Receive the Holy Spirit." It is the Spirit of Jesus, for Jesus himself promised to send the Spirit in his place. Ever since then, he has been the secret guide and guardian of the Church; from that time onward he has led the faithful into love and to God.

The Holy Spirit is himself a gift of God; indeed, he is the greatest and highest gift of God. That is why the sin against the Holy Spirit is the sin that cannot be forgiven (B → **Mt 12:31–32**); for this is the denial of God himself, the rejection of his love. We need to remind ourselves again and again: there are no half measures here—God himself gives himself to us in his love. Y → 120

Confirmation "increases the gifts of the Holy Spirit in us" as the *Catechism of the Catholic Church* tells us (**CCC 1203**). What do these gifts actually signify?

Wisdom is not some kind of secretive babble, nor is it a collection of sentimental sayings, such as one often finds in certain kinds of esoteric gift books. Instead, it is precisely the gift that transcends human wisdom and human counsels, the capacity to distinguish between the divine from the human. The gift of wisdom should enable us to recognize God and acquire a loving nature.

Understanding is the gift that helps us to understand our faith. Each of us should seek to penetrate farther into the truths of Christianity and learn to distinguish them from passing human knowledge and earthly attitudes.

With the gift of **counsel**, it is a question of decision-making. Often enough we find ourselves at a crossroads in life and do not know which way to go. We are confronted with means that are meant to serve a good end—but are these means good in themselves? We need constantly to scrutinize our own actions and those of our fellowmen: Is the spirit at work in them the Spirit of Jesus or that of another?

The gift of **fortitude** is not about being a macho or alpha male but, rather, about applying a genuine athlete's outlook to the realm of faith as well (see **B** → **Phil 3:14**). Single-mindedness, self-discipline, and training will lead to victory over the evil one. It is much easier, less challenging, and more "acceptable", so to speak, to go with the flow, to think and live in the way that the prevailing fashion or public opinion dictates. Faithfulness and strength of will are needed here—qualities we cannot supply alone and unaided.

Knowledge—"Science has shown …" No doubt you've heard the phrase before? Again and again we are told of "pioneering discoveries" that so often, on closer inspection, prove to be far less spectacular than we thought. Such supposed new "knowledge" and insights are no less familiar nowadays in the areas of faith and the Church. The gift of knowledge, therefore, is the gift of discernment: What is more plausible? What can I know? Modesty is also a scholarly virtue.

Piety does not get good press today—and yet in antiquity it was regarded as the highest of virtues. For it has nothing to do with preaching from the pulpit or praying in a convent; rather, it has to do with respect: for God and his laws, for nature, for our elders, for the feelings of others. But anyone who shows a lack of respect during religious worship is truly making himself ridiculous.

Fear of the Lord does not mean "being afraid of God" but, rather, "the beginning of wisdom" (**B** → **Sir 1:14**): It means a respect—indeed a reverence—for the divine that far exceeds all respect for created things. God is the Creator; God is the Lord over life and death, and God is the supreme Judge for all eternity. Understanding this sheer difference of degree and taking account of its importance in our actions is the first step toward true worship of God. In bestowing this gift on us, the Holy Spirit also teaches us its accompanying virtue, namely, humility.

LESSON

7

CATEGORY

The Holy Spirit—The Great Unknown

Theme and objective:
The Holy Spirit is the third Divine Person.
He gives us strength to live our life consciously with God.
We look more closely at the fruits of the Holy Spirit.

Preparation

For each of your students, buy a short but stubby white candle, and in addition buy nine sheets of wax in different colors. Cut up the wax sheets in such a way that each candidate has a sufficiently large piece in each color. Bear in mind also that each student should be able to use a pair of scissors, and think about protecting the surfaces in the room (for example, with something like newspaper).

Introduction

Play a game of "The Great Unknown" with your students. You impersonate an unknown person, and your students have to find out who it is by asking questions, to which you will only answer with "Yes" or "No". Needless to say, you will play the role of the "Holy Spirit". If you suspect that your students have already guessed the topic of the lesson, either by looking at their student books or because they are simply too smart, you can put them off the scent by first having one or two of the young people play some other person before you take your turn. In order to avoid any risk, it's probably best to prepare slips of paper with roles written on them beforehand for the two students who go first.

Link

Lead on to the next point like this: *"It's not only in this game that the Holy Spirit is "the great unknown". The truth is that many people don't really understand very well what the mysterious figure of the Holy Spirit is all about."*

Input—the Holy Spirit as a Divine Person

We suggest explaining the Holy Spirit like this:

"The Holy Spirit is just as much God as the Father and the Son. He 'proceeds from the Father and from the Son', as the Church declares in the Creed. He is the love that binds them both together. The Holy Spirit also binds us together with Jesus and binds all Christians together with one another.
In the Holy Spirit it becomes quite clear that our God is not a solitary God who exists for himself alone. Instead, God is, within himself, both love and community: Father and Son are united together in the Holy Spirit. This love, which is the Holy Spirit, is the gift that God wishes to give to us also."

Link

After giving this brief input—and clarifying any questions that may arise—ask the following question in order to lead on to the next point: *"The Holy Spirit is the third Divine Person. That's all well and good. But what does the Holy Spirit actually do in our lives?"*

Game: Keeping balloons in the air

Give each of the students an uninflated party balloon. The aim is to keep it up in the air as long as possible, without it touching the floor, but only by patting it briefly. The most skillful players might manage to keep it up in the air two or three times at most.

Then, of course, you play the game again, this time with the balloons inflated.

You can summarize the point of the game like this: "Without the Holy Spirit, we're like balloons without air in them. But when we are filled with the Holy Spirit, then we are ready to cope with the obstacles in life."

Bible session—The Story of Pentecost

Now read or retell the story of Pentecost, as it is told in Saint John's Gospel and the Acts of the Apostles (B → **Jn 20:19-22**—before they receive the Holy Spirit, the apostles barricade themselves in out of fear B → **Acts 1:1-12,37-38**). Alternatively you can read the two Bible passages together.

Discussion

Ask your students what they were able to identify as the effects of the Holy Spirit in the Pentecost account. The following aspects should emerge for discussion here:
- He strengthens us and drives away our fear
- He gives us the capacity to do things we could not have done without him
- He prepares our hearts to speak about Jesus

Link

Lead on now to your candle craft session, saying something like this: *"Let's look a little closer now at what the Holy Spirit can do in us. In his letter to the Galatians, Saint Paul speaks of the fruits of the Holy Spirit"* (B → **Gal 5:22-23**, see also Y → **311**).

Making a Holy Spirit candle

Assign one color in advance to each of the nine fruits of the Holy Spirit. Each member of the group is now given a white candle and nine wax sheets, one in each color. Talk to your candidates about the fruits of the Holy Spirit, one at a time. After each fruit, each person cuts out a flame shape from the appropriate wax sheet and presses it onto his white candle in such a way that in the end the image of a flame is created, composed of nine different flames. Ideally, you take the templates provided in the material as your model.

For your convenience, we have reprinted below the explanations on the fruits of the Holy Spirit that are given in the student's book.

NB: in YOUCAT Y → **311**, you will find all twelve fruits of the Holy Spirit listed. However, we restrict ourselves here to the nine mentioned by Saint Paul.

Conclusion and prayer

Breathe in me, O Holy Spirit

Breathe in me, O Holy Spirit,
that my thoughts may all be holy.
Act in me, O Holy Spirit,
that my work, too, may be holy.
Draw my heart, O Holy Spirit,
that I may love but what is holy.
Strengthen me, O Holy Spirit,
to defend all that is holy.
Guard me, then, O Holy Spirit,
that I may always be holy.
Amen.

SAINT AUGUSTINE OF HIPPO

LESSON

7

CATEGORY

The Holy Spirit—The Great Unknown

Theme and objective:
The Holy Spirit is the third Divine Person.
He gives us strength to live our life consciously with God.
We look more closely at the fruits of the Holy Spirit.

Introduction

Play a game of "The Great Unknown" with your students. You impersonate an unknown person, and your students have to find out who it is by asking questions, to which you will only answer with "Yes" or "No". Needless to say, you will play the role of the "Holy Spirit". If you suspect that your students have already guessed the topic of the lesson, either by looking at their student books or because they are simply too smart, you can put them off the scent by first having one or two of the young people play some other person before you take your turn. In order to avoid any risk, it's probably best to prepare slips of paper with roles written on them beforehand for the two students who go first.

Link

Lead on to the next point like this: *"It's not only in this game that the Holy Spirit is "the great unknown". The truth is that many people don't really understand very well what the mysterious figure of the Holy Spirit is all about."*

Input—the Holy Spirit as a Divine Person

We suggest explaining the Holy Spirit like this:
"The Holy Spirit is just as much God as the Father and the Son. He 'proceeds from the Father and from the Son', as the Church declares in the Creed. He is the love that binds them both together. The Holy Spirit also binds us together with Jesus and binds all Christians together with one another.
In the Holy Spirit it becomes quite clear that our God is not a solitary God who exists for himself alone. Instead, God is, within himself, both love and community: Father and Son are united together in the Holy Spirit. This love, which is the Holy Spirit, is the gift that God wishes to give to us men also."

Link

After giving this brief input—and clarifying any questions that may arise—ask the following question in order to lead on to the next point: *"The Holy Spirit is the third Divine Person. That's all well and good. But what does the Holy Spirit actually do in our lives?"*

Game: Keeping balloons in the air

Give each of the students an uninflated party balloon. The aim is to keep it up in the air as long as possible, without it touching the floor, but only by patting it briefly. The most skillful players might manage to keep it up in the air two or three times at most.

Then, of course, you play the game again, this time with the balloons inflated.

You can summarize the point of the game like this: *"Without the Holy Spirit, we're like balloons without air in them. But when we are filled with the Holy Spirit, then we are ready to cope with the obstacles in life."*

BIBLE SESSION—THE STORY OF PENTECOST

Now read together the story of Pentecost, as it is told in Saint John's Gospel and the Acts of the Apostles (B → **Jn 20:19–22**—before they receive the Holy Spirit, the apostles barricade themselves in out of fear B → **Acts 1:1–12,37–38**).

DISCUSSION

Ask your students what they were able to identify as the effects of the Holy Spirit in the Pentecost account. The following aspects should emerge for discussion here:

- He strengthens us and drives away our fear
- He gives us the capacity to do things we could not have done without him
- He prepares our hearts to speak about Jesus

Link

"Let's look a little closer now at what the Holy Spirit can do in us. In his letter to the Galatians, Saint Paul speaks of the fruits of the Holy Spirit" (B → **Gal 5:22–23**; see also Y → **311**).

The Fruits of the Holy Spirit

Discuss together with your students the fruits of the Holy Spirit. You can either photocopy explanations from the material opposite, or else they can read them directly out of the student's book (also at youcatconfirmation.com). The best approach here is to read out each of the fruits in turn and then discuss it together.

NB: In the YOUCAT Y → 311 you will find all twelve fruits of the Holy Spirit listed. However, we will restrict ourselves here to the nine mentioned by Saint Paul.

Conclusion and prayer

Breathe in me, O Holy Spirit

Breathe in me, O Holy Spirit,
that my thoughts may all be holy.
Act in me, O Holy Spirit,
that my work, too, may be holy.
Draw my heart, O Holy Spirit,
that I may love but what is holy.
Strengthen me, O Holy Spirit,
to defend all that is holy.
Guard me, then, O Holy Spirit,
that I may always be holy.
Amen.

SAINT AUGUSTINE OF HIPPO

LOVE (CHARITY)

Wherever the Holy Spirit is, there is Love. Love is more than mere feelings. Otherwise, we could only love an utterly sweet little baby. But we should love all babies, even the ugly or deformed ones. When the Holy Spirit kindles the love of God within us, then it's a bit like plugging into the power socket. You feel within you all the feelings that God himself has for what he has created—the people, the animals, the flowers. God is crazy with love for us. And God's love is unconditional, with no ifs and whens; it is not a passing love; it "never ends". It is utterly faithful. It transforms everything, above all the world of your relationships. With God's love inside you, you see everything with new eyes.

JOY

Wherever the Holy Spirit is, there is joy. Imagine a rock concert where everyone is rejoicing, dancing, waving his arms, jumping in the air. Jesus has defeated death. How cool is that, then? We are redeemed! Paradise is waiting for us. We can dance for joy, even if we still have any number of problems on our shoulders. In heaven, they tell us, the angels dance. And there is greater joy over one single person who converts and leaves all his sins behind him "than over ninety-nine righteous persons".

PEACE

Wherever the Holy Spirit is, there is peace. All inner unrest ceases. Sadness sinks away. Fear subsides. You find your inner balance and are no longer driven about by your passions, like a leaf in the wind. Other people seek your company and your friendship because you are in harmony with yourself and with other people—and even with the animals. The peace in your heart makes you totally likeable.

PATIENCE

Wherever the Holy Spirit is, there is patience. Patience means having the courage to play the long game. Where others throw in the towel, you can find that extra stamina. The rapid burnout was yesterday's game. Where once you had the lungs for 800 meters, now you're a marathon runner. You can shrug off setbacks as if they're nothing. The Holy Spirit makes you into a fighter who never quits. Other people wonder where you get the strength. But you know.

KINDNESS

Wherever the Holy Spirit is, there is kindness. You hold the door open for someone else. You help other people with their homework. You practice in secret with someone who always bungles his volleyball serve. Mother Teresa was always reminding her sisters, who cared for the dying: "It's not enough just to care for them; you must do so with a smile!"

GOODNESS

Wherever the Holy Spirit is, there is goodness. God is all good. Doing good puts us close to God. Anyone who continually does good is automatically a "good" person—that is to say, habitually good to others. You talk to the dropout on the street corner, buy a newspaper from him. You help a child, talk to a lonely person. You spend a long time listening to an old person. You take an interest in other people's cares and worries. Living a life of goodness is the "life-style" of God. When people are with a good person, they can relax and blossom.

FAITHFULNESS

Wherever the Holy Spirit is, there is faithfulness. God does not change from day to day. You can count on him 100%, even when your prayers to him are sometimes answered in a rather different way than you had originally hoped. He is faithful to you, even if you betray him and other people a thousand times over. The Holy Spirit helps you to become firm-hearted and "faithful until death"—a true image of the faithful God. Have you ever read the book *The Little Prince*, by Saint-Exupéry? There is a wonderful phrase in it about faithfulness: "You become responsible forever for what you have befriended."

GENTLENESS

Wherever the Holy Spirit is, there is gentleness. What this fruit of the Holy Spirit means is that you will have courage, but a tender courage that is not violent and does not, even in a good cause, destroy rather than build up; instead, it heals and achieves something beautiful. So you will have courage, but combined with love and patience. To bring about something great in loving patience—that is the kind of boldness that God loves. Jesus redeemed the world through a particular kind of boldness—he walked the path of nonviolence all the way to the Cross.

SELF CONTROL

Where the Holy Spirit is, there is self-control. The Holy Spirit within you enables you to be fully yourself. You will no longer be possessed by things that hold you prisoner, by people who have kept you in a state of dependency, by powerful people who order you about. You will no longer be driven by your desires, no longer be the slave of your passions. You will be free to do what your heart truly desires to do, namely, the good for which God has created you.

8 Prayer—staying in touch with the living God

Theological basis

"Lord, teach us to pray", the disciples asked Jesus (B → Lk 11:1). We could once again ask, as in chapter 1, what there is to learn. For after all, God will hardly sit there grinning when he hears our prayer, and then shake his head like a teacher and say, "That's not really important ... and will not be answered." Or is he? Well, yes and no. For everyone has sometimes experienced the fact that God does not seem to answer every prayer. But why not? Did he not say, "Ask, and it will be given you" (B → Mt 7:7)? Yet, to ask a counterquestion, what kind of a God would it be who simply does everything we can think of to ask? A kind of "wish-granting" machine? Y → 469

Our faith teaches us that God is free and that he keeps his own counsel. We can't simply look over his shoulder to see what he plans for us; we do not necessarily know what is best for us. Not everyone can win the lottery ... (In the film *Bruce Almighty,* Bruce Nolan is allowed to play God. In fact, *Bruce Almighty* gives everyone what they ask for and ends up creating total chaos.)

Obviously, we can wish for plainly unchristian, unacceptable things. Anyone who has evil motives need not bother turning to God (B → Ps 66:18; Jas 4:3). We sometimes hear of people who ask God for a new car, even for a particular model. Whether and how God will respond to such purely materialistic wishes or requests for luxury items is hard to say (that's something that might even backfire ...). Similarly, an attitude of carelessness, complacency, or cowardice is scarcely an appropriate background for God's kindness. Though when it comes to our own imperfections and limitations, it is a rather different matter.

What surely matters most is to have the right attitude in prayer (B → Jn 15:7). This is not something we can simply separate from the rest of our lives (B → Mic 3:2–4), let alone from the declared will of God (B → 1 Cor 4:7) are virtues we should bring to prayer. Prayer is a conversation with God, not simply a matter of posting a ready-made wish list and then waiting for the results. It would be a misunderstanding of prayer to expect only to change God's mind, without including the willingness, on the part of the supplicant, to change himself.

In the Christian faith and life—and also when talking to God—we should expect to have other priorities and wishes than those with a purely worldly perspective (B → Mt 6:19–34, 5:44–45). That is why, when Jesus responds to the request of his disciples (B → Lk 11:1), he gives them the Our Father. The Our Father (B → Mt 6:9–13; Lk 11:2–4) is **the** prayer. Y → 511–527

We should always ask that our prayer may be answered in accordance with the will of God. The perfect example of this is Jesus himself during his agony in the Garden of Gethsemane: "My Father, if it be possible, let this chalice pass from me; nevertheless, not as I will, but as you will" (B → Mt 26:39). Even when God's answer does not correspond to the pattern of "I wish—God fulfills", or "I command—God obeys", but only to the will of God, who loves us and knows all things (B → Is 55:8).

And now, after all these things have been considered and borne in mind, we should pray with joyful hope and faith that our prayer will be fulfilled (B → Jas 1:6–8, Mk 11:24), even when God's answer does not correspond to the pattern of "I wish—God fulfills", or "I command—God obeys", but only to the will of God, who loves us and knows all things (B → Ps 139:1–7,23).

Moreover, we should not only pray when things go wrong. If our personal relationship with God consists of nothing more than phoning God up like an emergency doctor, then it is a selfish and negligent kind of attitude. We should think of prayer to the Holy Spirit, we should seek his counsel, and we should also thank God, even when we have not prayed to him; we should examine ourselves self-critically before him, ask his pardon, pray for our fellowmen (as we do in the intercessory prayers at Holy Mass). There is so much that we ourselves cannot provide, things we simply owe to God: our gifts and talents, our family home, the world around us, our friendships, our faith, our joyful moments, etc. Hence there is every reason to go through life in an attitude of joyful gratitude and to express this joy and gratitude again and again to our God. Y → 498–499

Prayer—Talking with God

Theme and objective:
Prayer is a friendly conversation with God.
The posture we adopt and certain outward forms help us avoid distraction in prayer.

Preparation

- Copy the opening words of the four psalms from the material provided below onto four separate sheets of paper. Don't forget to provide paper and pencils.
- Get a crucifix for shared prayer. If you would like to have some gentle music playing in the background, then don't forget to provide the appropriate music player.
- Get some small wooden tablets, one for each student, plus a sufficient quantity of gold paint, glue, and decorative stones or tiles. Have, in advance (!), a copy of an icon of Jesus for each student—for example, the icon of the "Glorified Christ".
- Alternatively, provide each student with a photocopy of the cross of San Damiano (available at youcatconfirmation .com), together with a sufficient quantity of stiff cardboard, felt-tip pens, scissors, and glue.

Introduction

Begin the lesson with a warm-up game (about distraction). Divide the group into several teams. Each team consists of a messenger and one or more receivers. The messengers are given one of the four sheets with the opening words of the psalms on them, while the receivers are given paper and a pencil. The messengers have to stand in one corner of the room, the receivers in the opposite one. All the messengers have to shout out the words on their own sheet—at the same time—while the receivers try to write them down, without any mistakes. The aim of the game, therefore, is to concentrate, to listen very carefully, and not to let oneself be distracted by the noise of the others.

Link

You can now link this to today's theme by saying: *"It's the same with prayer. Very often we let ourselves be distracted by external, unimportant things. Saint Francis de Sales has given us a useful and interesting tip in this regard. He tells us that all the great saints, for whom prayer was so important, believed that a reverent posture, such as kneeling, folding our hands together, or crossing our arms over our chest, makes a very big difference. This attitude, or posture, of prayer helps us, in a way we would not have imagined, to remain recollected in God's presence and focused on him. (See also the quotations in* Y → **p. 268 f.***) So now we're going to try out a few different prayer postures together."*

Trying out different postures of prayer

Place a crucifix on the floor, and arrange the students, with their chairs, in a semicircle around it. If you wish, you can at the same time play gentle and peaceful music in the background. Now try out the following typical prayer postures together:

1 Standing, with hands joined
2 Standing, with arms outstretched (the orans posture)
3 Sitting
4 Kneeling
5 Kneeling back on the heels
6 Kneeling, bent forward

Let your students try out each posture for around a minute or so, in order to feel its impact; then you can talk together about the effect each position had on them (see also the prayer postures in Y → **p. 268**).

Input prayer

Explain to your students that prayer is a conversation with God. Remind them of the following aspects:

- When we pray, we can speak to God as we would to a friend.
- We can tell him all our cares.
- We can ask him for help and advice.
- We can turn to him at any time.

Remind your students, though, that we can't always expect to hear God's answer immediately. Sometimes that may be because we let ourselves be distracted and don't listen properly, but it may well also be for reasons that remain hidden from us.

This is a good moment to talk about and share our personal experience of prayer. Make sure that no one feels pressured into talking about things he would rather keep to himself.

A brief look at the Little School of Prayer
Together look at and discuss nos. 2, 3, and 4 of the YOUCAT Little School of Prayer. You can find this in the YOUCAT Confirmation book or in the YOUCAT prayer book. It is also reprinted again in the study materials in this teacher's handbook.

Link
No. 4 in the school of prayer suggests that you prepare a place in which to pray. For such a prayer corner, it is appropriate to have an image of Jesus or a crucifix, and this is what you can now work on together.

Making a crucifix or an icon of Jesus
In the more simple variant, each candidate makes his own cross. Each student is given a copy of the cross of San Damiano, which he can then embellish himself. Afterward it is glued onto a piece of stiff cardboard and cut to shape, so that each candidate now has a cross of his own for a private prayer corner.
In the somewhat more elaborate version, wooden boards are first of all painted or sprayed with gold paint. Then the icon image is glued in the center of this "gilded" board. The resulting gold frame can then be further decorated with gemstones, etc., so that each candidate now has his own icon of Jesus.

Conclusion and prayer
Our Father who art in heaven,
hallowed be thy name;
thy kingdom come,
thy will be done
on earth as it is in heaven.
Give us this day our daily bread,
and forgive us our trespasses,
as we forgive those who trespass against us;
and lead us not into temptation,
but deliver us from evil.
For the kingdom, the power and the glory are yours,
now and for ever.
Amen.

LESSON

8

CATEGORY

Prayer—Talking with God

Theme and objective:
Prayer is a friendly conversation with God.
The posture we adopt and certain outward forms help us avoid distraction in prayer.

Preparation

- Copy the opening words of the four psalms from the material provided below onto four separate sheets of paper. Don't forget to provide paper and pencils.
- Copy the list of five "fictional prayers" for each student.
- Make copies of the "Little School of Prayer" for each student, or else have them bring it with them, in their Student's book or in the YOUCAT prayer book.
- Copy the "Suggestions for your own prayers" for each student.

Introduction

Begin the lesson with a warm-up game (about distraction). Divide the group into several teams. Each team consists of a messenger and one or more receivers. The messengers are given one of the four sheets with the opening words of the psalm on them, while the receivers are given paper and a pencil. The messengers have to stand in one corner of the room, the receivers in the opposite one. All the messengers have to shout out the words on their own sheet—at the same time—while the receivers try to write them down, without any mistakes. The aim of the game, therefore, is to concentrate, to listen very carefully, and not to let oneself be distracted by the noise of the others.

Link

You can now link this to today's theme by saying: "It's the same with prayer. Very often we let ourselves be distracted by external, unimportant things."

Input prayer

Explain to your students that prayer is a conversation with God. Remind them of the following aspects:

- When we pray, we can speak to God as we would to a friend.
- We can tell him all our cares.
- We can ask him for help and advice.
- We can turn to him at any time.

Remind your students, though, that we can't always expect to hear God's answer immediately. Sometimes that may be because we let ourselves be distracted and don't listen properly, but it may well also be for reasons that remain hidden from us.

Some fictional prayers

Take a look with your group at the following five made-up prayers from the worksheet materials provided, and talk about them together. You can hand out the prayers individually to your students, on a strip of paper, and get volunteers to read aloud the situation and the prayer. Go through the prayers one at a time, and give the youngsters an opportunity to say what they think about each individual prayer.

In school, David feels excluded. The other boys are constantly picking on him and making fun of him. David is the one who gets the blame for everything. Lena has been aware of this for some time and feels sorry for David. So she prays, "Jesus, please make them not treat David so badly."

Alex is determined to get himself a new computer game. So he takes some money from the drawer in his father's writing desk and buys the game. That night he prays, "Dear God, help me, and make Dad not notice it!"

Mrs. Brewer is eighty-four and has suffered for years from a painful illness. Often she is in severe pain all day long. She constantly prays, "O Jesus, give me back my health, or at least take away this pain. But not my will, but your will be done."

Evelyn can't stand math in school. She regularly copies her homework from her friend. When an exam looms, she decides to try praying: "God, help me to get a B." So when she gets an F, she quickly decides: "Prayer doesn't work."

Jack once saw a program on TV about the street children in Brazil. Ever since then, he has prayed every day that people will help these children.

In your discussion, you should note the following things: With Lena, Mrs. Brewer, and Jack, there is absolutely nothing to be faulted in their prayers. However, prayer should not stop them from also trying to do whatever they can themselves about the situation.

Evelyn quite plainly confuses prayer with a sort of magic ritual for getting what she wants. And of course that's not the way it works. Prayer is not a substitute for hard work on our part.

Alex, in his prayer, is actually trying to make God into his accomplice after having stolen the money. That is not a good idea. However, it could just be the beginning of a step in the right direction, if he at least recognizes that he has done wrong and sincerely wants to put things right.

YOUCAT Little School of Prayer

Divide into three or four smaller groups, each of which will look at two or three of the suggestions and then, after ten minutes or so, present them to the rest of the group. If there are any points still left over, you can either entrust them to a small group of the brightest pupils or else deal with them yourself.

Discussion

Go chronologically through each of the numbered suggestions. Let each group of students first of all present the point themselves, and then give the rest of the group the opportunity to express their views. This would also be a good moment to introduce your own prayer experiences into the discussion.

Writing a prayer of our own

Now give your students some time to write out a prayer by themselves. In doing so, the following suggestions may be of help to them. Tell them beforehand that their prayer will not be read aloud but will remain something between God and themselves.

- Prayer naturally always begins with some form of address. You can choose this according to your personal relationship with God. In fact, there are no obligatory forms. But you should never be disrespectful, of course. After all, you are speaking to God himself. Typical forms of address are: "Dear God", "Jesus", or "Lord".
- It is good to begin your prayer with a brief word of praise or thanksgiving.
- Tell God quite simply about your life, about your joys, your fears, or your worries.
- Entrust your intentions and petitions to him.
- Is there anyone you know, or know of, who is in any kind of need or suffering? Think of him, too, in your prayer.
- No doubt there are many things in your life for which you can and would like to give thanks. There is room in your prayer for gratitude, also.
- Maybe not everything you did in recent days was as good as it should have been. Prayer is also an opportunity to ask God's forgiveness for whatever you've done wrong.
- We normally conclude our prayers with the word "Amen". It means something like, "Yes, may it be that way."

Conclusion and prayer

Our Father who art in heaven,
hallowed be thy name;
thy kingdom come,
thy will be done
on earth as it is in heaven.
Give us this day our daily bread,
and forgive us our trespasses,
as we forgive those who trespass against us;
and lead us not into temptation,
but deliver us from evil.
For the kingdom, the power and the glory are yours, now and for ever.
Amen.

Little School of Prayer

Make the decision.

God willed and created us to be free human beings. Many times a day we deliberate, set priorities, make decisions. Without decisions, nothing gets done. If you want to, make the decision to become a praying person and to shape your relationship to God. Decide deliberately ahead of time: I will pray at such and such a time. In the evening, make the decision to pray morning prayer, and in the morning to pray evening prayer.

Be faithful in little things.

Many begin to pray with great resolutions. After a while, they fail and think they cannot pray at all. Begin with definite, short prayer times. And keep doing it faithfully. Then your longing and your prayer, too, can grow, as it is appropriate for you, your time, and the circumstances.

Take time to pray.

Praying means being alert to the fact that God is interested in me. With him, you do not have to schedule appointments. There are three criteria for the time of your prayer that can be helpful. Choose set times (habit helps), quiet times (this is often early morning and in the evening), and valuable time that you like but are willing to give away as a gift (no "spare moments").

Prepare a place.

The place where you pray has its effect on your praying. Therefore, look for a place where you can pray well. For many people, this will be at the bedside or the desk. Others find it helpful when they have a specially prepared place that reminds and invites them: a place that has a stool or a chair with a kneeler, a carpet, an icon or picture, a candle, the Bible, a prayer book.

Rituals give structure to your prayer life.

Having to make yourself settle down to prayer every time can be a great expense of energy. Give your prayer a fixed order (a ritual). This is not supposed to restrict you but is meant, rather, to help you, so that you do not have to deliberate every day whether and how you want to pray. Before prayer, place yourself consciously in the presence of God; after prayer, take another moment to thank God for his blessings and to place yourself under his protection.

Let the whole person pray.

Praying is accomplished not only in thoughts and words. In prayer, the whole person can be united with God: your body, your internal and external perception, your memory, your will, your thoughts and feelings, or the dream from last night. Even distractions often give you important information about what really concerns and motivates you and what you can intentionally bring into God's presence and leave with him. When things you need to do and don't want to forget occur to you while you're praying, you can write them down and then go back to praying.

Pray in a variety of ways.

Discover and practice the many ways of praying, which can vary depending on the time, one's frame of mind, and the present situation: a prayer composed by someone else with which I join in; personal prayer about my own concerns; praying with a passage from Sacred Scripture (for example, the readings for the day); the prayer of the heart (or "Jesus Prayer"), in which a short prayer formula or simply the name "Jesus" is repeated with each breath; interior prayer, in which the whole person is silent and listens internally and externally.

Use the opportunities.

You can also make use of the opportunities that arise to pray at in-between times (for example, short, fervent prayers, a petition, a prayer of thanksgiving or praise): while waiting, while riding on a bus, a train, or in a car (instead of turning the music on right away), during free time, while visiting a chapel or church along your daily walk. Let the opportunities you have to pray become invitations to unite yourself again and again with God.

Let God speak.

Praying also means listening to God's voice. God speaks most explicitly in the words of Sacred Scripture, which the Church reads day after day. He speaks through the Tradition of the Church and the witness of the saints. But he also speaks—often in a hidden way—in the heart of every man, for instance in the judgment of your conscience or through an interior joy. God's Word in Scripture makes it possible to hear the Word of God in the heart and lends a voice to it. Give God a chance to speak in your prayer. Become familiar with him, so that you can learn to tell his voice apart from the many other voices and come to know his will.

Pray with the Church on earth and in heaven

Anyone who prays—whether alone or with others—enters into the great community of those who pray. It extends from earth to heaven and includes those who are alive today and also the angels, the saints, and the unknown multitude of those who live with God. Praying also means praying for each other. Therefore, it is good to pray not only by yourself but also, when possible, with others: with your family, with friends, with your congregation—and with the saints. You can ask them for their prayers. For in God's sight the community of those who pray does not cease with death.

Blessed is the man who walks not in the counsel of the wicked, nor stands in the way of sinners, nor sits in the seat of scoffers; but his delight is in the law of the LORD, and on his law he meditates day and night.

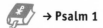 → Psalm 1

Why do the nations conspire and the peoples plot in vain? The kings of the earth set themselves, and the rulers take counsel together, against the LORD and his anointed, saying, "Let us burst their bonds asunder, and cast their cords from us."

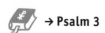 → Psalm 2

O LORD, how many are my foes! Many are rising against me; many are saying of me, there is no help for him in God. But you, O LORD, are a shield about me, my glory, and the lifter of my head.

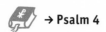 → Psalm 3

Answer me when I call, O God of my right! You have given me room when I was in distress. Be gracious to me, and hear my prayer. O sons of men, how long will you be dull of heart? How long will you love vain words, and seek after lies?

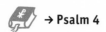 → Psalm 4

Prayers

In school, **David** feels excluded. The other boys are constantly picking on him and making fun of him. David is the one who gets the blame for everything. Lena has been aware of this for some time and feels sorry for David. So she prays, "Jesus, please make them not treat David so badly."

Alex is determined to get himself a new computer game. So he takes some money from the drawer in his father's writing desk and buys the game. That night he prays, "Dear God, help me, and make Dad not notice it!"

Mrs. Brewer is eighty-four and has suffered for years from a painful illness. Often she is in severe pain all day long. She constantly prays, "O Jesus, give me back my health, or at least take away this pain. But not my will, but your will be done."

Evelyn can't stand math in school. She regularly copies her homework from her friend. When an exam looms, she decides to try praying: "God, help me to get a B." So when she gets an F, she quickly decides: "Prayer doesn't work."

Jack once saw a program on TV about the street children in Brazil. Ever since then, he has prayed every day that people will help these children.

Some suggestions for our own prayers

- Prayer naturally always begins with some form of address. You can choose this according to your personal relationship with God. In fact, there are no obligatory forms. But you should never be disrespectful, of course. After all, you are speaking to God himself. Typical forms of address are: "Dear God", "Jesus", or "Lord".

- It is good to begin your prayer with a brief word of praise or thanksgiving.

- Tell God quite simply about your life, about your joys, your fears, or your worries.

- Entrust your intentions and petitions to him.

- Is there anyone you know, or know of, who is in any kind of need or suffering? Think of him, too, in your prayer.

- No doubt there are many things in your life for which you can and would like to give thanks. There is room in your prayer for gratitude, also.

- Maybe not everything you did in recent days was as good as it should have been. Prayer is also an opportunity to ask God's forgiveness for whatever you've done wrong.

- We normally conclude our prayers with the word "Amen". It means something like, "Yes, may it be that way."

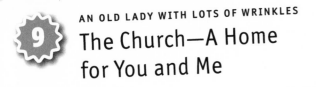
The Church—A Home for You and Me

Theological basis

Catholic Christians often have to cope with all kinds of criticisms—about the Inquisition, the Crusades, Galileo, etc. It is worth reading some decent books on the subject, such as Christopher Kaczor's *The Seven Big Myths about the Catholic Church*, or Walter Brandmüller's *Light and Shadows: Church History and Faith, Fact, and Legend* to help you give some answers to the worst of these prejudices. However, in many cases we simply have to hold up our hands and say, "Yes, unfortunately that's true." In the Holy Year 2000, Pope John Paul II made a great act of confession and asked for forgiveness for the sins committed by representatives of the Church over the course of her history. The fact is, the Church is not a club for the perfect, and membership in the Church doesn't automatically make us into saints. Never in the course of history, and not today.

However, many of the criticisms are not so much directed at the failings of individuals; rather, they arise from a crude misunderstanding. "There are not a hundred people in America who hate the Catholic Church. There are millions who hate what they wrongly believe to be the Catholic Church", said Archbishop Fulton Sheen, who died in 1979.

Indeed, the image of the Church that many of the media convey, and that many people likewise have in their heads, is terribly distorted—and unfair. We can't and won't go into detail here, as that would take a book in itself. There are just three general points: first of all, every one of us is a sinner, including those who are members of the Catholic Church. And the fact that people hold a particular office or rank in the Church doesn't mean they stop being sinners. Secondly, in this sense, the Church is always a child of her time. And although she has a different origin, different sources, and a different Lord, even the baptized understand no more of this than can be humanly understood from the perspective of their own times. And thirdly, those who criticize the Church are no less sinful and no less fallible than those they criticize. This can be demonstrated by a genuinely thorough and fair-minded study of Church history and Catholic Church teaching, from which it emerges that most of the criticisms and most of the prejudices are either baseless or taken out of their historical context.

This critical, or overcritical, picture of the Church frequently arises because people judge her according to analogies that are simply inaccurate.

- For example, the Church is not like a nation state. So why should she have to be a democracy? Is an orchestra a democracy, for example? And are we always in agreement with everything our own nation decides, simply because it springs from a democratic process? Can people decide the truth by a vote?
- Again, the Church is not like a commercial business. So why should she behave according to marketing laws? If a product no longer sells well, a company simply takes it off the market. And if it wants a product to sell, it has to make it look attractive by means of advertising. Is the Church supposed to try to sell Jesus to us as if we were customers?
- Finally, the Church is not like some comfy sofa, meant to cushion us from every harsh reality. If we want to relax and have fun, we can go and play in the park. But if we want to get fit or run a marathon, then we have to train hard. Do we want God to be our trainer, or our entertainer?

YOUCAT summarizes well what the Church is:

The Church is more than an institution because she is a **mystery** that is simultaneously human and divine. Y → 124

The Church is the Body of Christ. That means we are not simply "paying members in the Friends of Jesus Club"; rather, we are the body of the God-made-man on earth. The Head of this body is Christ himself. Y → 121

The life-giving principle of the Church is the Spirit of Christ. It is he who has spoken through the prophets, who is at work in the sacraments, who lives in the hearts of the faithful, and who speaks in their prayers. Y → 128

The Church does not exist for herself. Nor is she there so that individuals can simply please themselves and think only about their own self-fulfillment. Y → 122

The Church is the People of God, called into being by God himself, led by Jesus Christ, and with the Holy Spirit as the source of her life. Y → 125

Equally, as the People of God, the Church does not exist for her own ends. There is a saying, "A Church that does not serve, serves no purpose." It would be a mistake to see the Church as a means of fulfilling any kind of particular interests—in some cases, interests that profoundly contradict the commandments of God and the mission of the Church. But the Church does not exist for her own ends. Y → 123

If we simply consider these three points and bear them in mind, then it becomes clear that the Church cannot be compared with a state, a club, or a commercial company, because she belongs to two different spheres—in short, she is both divine and human at once. Certainly, she bears the outward characteristics of an institution, but anyone who regards her purely in this light has misunderstood her nature. She is the body whose Head is Christ and whose members we are. And this reality is brought about by the Holy Spirit, in faith, in the sacraments.

Yet this is a joint mission, not a solitary one. It is a mission accomplished in relationship, just as God himself exists in relationship. And it is accomplished in loving service toward that which is not Church. A work of mission, a social mission. It has been summarized very beautifully as follows: "That is why the Church, for all her weakness, is a formidable bit of heaven on earth." Y → 123

What is important to convey, then, is that we must not cultivate a one-sided view of the Church but must instead be ourselves present and active within her, must be Church together. For, in many cases, these images of the Church as a monolithic block arise from the fact that we ourselves are far too little active within her and, instead, see her far too much from the outside. Undoubtedly, this perspective can be necessary from time to time, for we have seen that the Church is outward looking and should not be constantly navel-gazing. But that is not how we recognize her inner reality, her true nature. We discover this in prayer, in the reception of the sacraments, in reading the Sacred Scriptures, in Christian communion, and in the spreading of the faith.

"Everyone can make a start, even if he is filthy or simply feels dirty, is deeply in debt, cannot cope with his emotions, lives in an irregular relationship, or has more questions than answers. Even if he is divorced, for the third, fourth, fifth time, if he is an alcoholic, a drug addict, or an Internet addict (or all three at once); if he once believed but has lost his faith in the turmoil of life. It does not matter. Becoming a Christian does not presuppose that you are already living correctly, as though you had to put your life in order before you could let God see you. If that were so, no one would ever become a Christian. For who can claim that his life is already perfect?"

BERNHARD MEUSER, *Christsein für Einsteiger*, p. 17

What's the Church about?

CATEGORY

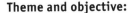

Theme and objective:
The Church is the "Body of Christ," in which each of us has his own particular task.
Priests have a special vocation in the Church.
We are all called to follow Christ, as part of the Church.

Preparation
- Provide paper and pencils. Don't forget to bring your cell phone or your watch if you want to stop exactly on time.
- Photocopy the worksheets "We are Church" (p. 73), and cut them to size. Buy a big bag of jelly beans, and bring a bowl and a pair of scissors as well.
- Photocopy the page showing the structure of the Catholic Church (p. 74 or download at youcatconfirmation.com).

Introduction

Give your students precisely three minutes to write down as many words as possible that could be used instead of the word "Church".

Link

Shock your students by telling them that we can also call the Church the "Body of Christ".

Group work

Divide your students up into three groups. Their task will be to read **B** → **1 Cor 12:12–31a Y** → **126** (the Church as the Body of Christ) and to try and summarize why the Church is also called the "Body of Christ".

Presentation of the results

Let the groups present their findings, and give everyone an opportunity to ask questions.

Game: "We are Church"

As a warm-up and introduction to the theme "one body, but many members", play the game "We are Church" with your students. Before you start, hide the jelly beans next to the window, the scissors in the wastebasket, and the bowl in the cupboard (unless you have adapted the instruction slips accordingly). Give out the instruction slips to the students, and explain to them that their collective task is to put the bowl on the table, to open a bag of jelly beans with the scissors, and to pour the jelly beans into the bowl. But they must strictly observe the rules on their instruction slips.

NB: The first part is that of the coordinator and, hence, a particularly important one. So make sure you give this to a suitable pupil.

DISCUSSION

When the game is over and you are eating the jelly beans together, talk to your students about the way the game works, and show the connection with the Church as the Body of Christ, as described in the First Letter to the Corinthians ("one body, many members")—assuming your group hasn't already spotted the connection for themselves.

Link

Explain to your group that the coordinator has a particularly important role—although in fact every individual role is also absolutely essential for success. Within the Church, the priest exercises a similar function, as the leader of the community.

YOUCAT SESSION

Together read **Y** → **138** (How is the one, holy, catholic, and apostolic Church structured?)

Group work

Divide your candidates into smaller groups of approximately three members, and give them roughly fifteen minutes to illustrate the structure of the Church, graphically. Then afterward you can come together and compare their results with the picture we have provided for you in the teaching materials.

DISCUSSION

Explain to your students that the word "Church" comes from the Greek word kyriake ("belonging to the Lord"), in other words, it includes all those who belong to Jesus (see also YOUCAT **Y** → **p. 77**). If necessary, emphasize again here that, while there are indeed different roles and services within the Church, all her members belong equally to Jesus and are called to follow him.

Discuss together what belonging to the Church and to Jesus means to you and where you see your place in the Church.

Conclusion and prayer

Heavenly Father,
we are your Church. You have called us to follow you and build up your kingdom together with you.
Give us your Spirit, so that in our lives we may listen to your voice and stay faithful to you.
Amen.

What's the Church about?

Theme and objective:
The Church is the "Body of Christ", in which each of us has his own particular task.
Priests have a special vocation in the Church.
We are all called to follow Christ, as part of the Church.

Preparation
- Provide paper and pencils. Don't forget to bring your cell phone or your watch if you want to stop exactly on time.
- Photocopy the worksheet "We are Church", and cut the copies to size. Buy a big bag of jelly beans, and bring a bowl and a pair of scissors as well.
- Photocopy the page showing the structure of the Catholic Church (p. 74 or download at youcatconfirmation.com).

Introduction
Give your students three minutes to write down as many words as possible that could be used instead of the word "Church".

Link
Shock your students by telling them that we can also call the Church the "Body of Christ", the "Temple of the Holy Spirit", and the "People of God".

Group work
Divide your students up into three groups. Each group must find and explain a designation for the Church, with the help of YOUCAT and the New Testament.

Group 1: **B → 1 Cor 12:12–31a** and   **Y → 126** (the Church as the Body of Christ)
Group 2: **B → 2 Cor 6:16** and   **Y → 128** (the Church as the Temple of the Holy Spirit)
Group 3: **B → 1 Pet 2:9–10** and   **Y → 125** (the Church as the People of God)

Presentation of the results
Let the groups present their findings, and give everyone an opportunity to ask questions.

Game: "We are Church"
As a warm-up and introduction to the theme "one body, but many members", play the game "We are Church" with your students. Before you start, hide the jelly beans next to the window, the scissors in the wastebasket, and the bowl in the cupboard (unless you have adapted the instruction slips accordingly). Give out the instruction slips to the students, and explain to them that their collective task is to put the bowl on the table, to open a bag of jelly beans with the scissors, and to pour the jelly beans into the bowl. But they must strictly observe the rules on their instruction slips.

NB: The first part is that of the coordinator and, hence, a particularly important one. So make sure you give this to a suitable pupil.

DISCUSSION
When the game is over and you are eating the jelly beans together, talk to your students about the way the game works, and show the connection with the Church as the Body of Christ, as described in the First Letter to the Corinthians ("one body, many members")—assuming your group hasn't already spotted the connection for themselves.

Link
Explain to your group that the coordinator has a particularly important role—although in fact every individual role is absolutely essential for success. Within the Church, the priest exercises a similar function, as the leader of the community.

YOUCAT Session

Together read Y → **138** (How is the one, holy, catholic, and apostolic Church structured?)

Group work

Divide your candidates into smaller groups of approximately three members, and give them roughly ten minutes to illustrate the structure of the Church graphically. Then afterward you can come together and compare their results with the picture we have provided for you in the teaching materials.

DISCUSSION

Explain to your students that the word "Church" comes from the Greek word *kyriake* ("belonging to the Lord"), in other words, it includes all those who belong to Jesus (see also YOUCAT Y → **p. 77**). If necessary, emphasize again here that, while there are indeed different roles and services within the Church, all her members belong equally to Jesus and are called to follow him.

Discuss together what belonging to the Church and to Jesus means to you and where you see your place in the Church.

Conclusion and prayer

Heavenly Father,
we are your Church.
You have called us to follow you and build up your kingdom together with you.
Give us your Spirit, so that in our lives we may listen to your voice and stay faithful to you.
Amen.

Game: "We are Church"

Your task is to put the bowl on the table, open the packet of jelly beans with the scissors, and pour the jelly beans into the bowl.

- -

You must not move an inch, and you mustn't touch anything. But you can talk as much as you want.

- -

You must not move an inch, and you mustn't touch anything. You are not allowed to say anything except "Yes", "No", "Me", and "Not me". The jelly beans are next to the window.

- -

You must not move an inch, and you mustn't touch anything. You are not allowed to say anything except "Yes", "No", "Me", and "Not me". The scissors are in the wastebasket.

- -

You must not move an inch, and you mustn't touch anything. You are not allowed to say anything except "Yes", "No", "Me", and "Not me". The bowl is in the cupboard.

- -

You can move only when you know exactly where the jelly beans, the bowl, and the scissors are located. You can carry only one item at a time. You are not allowed to use any of the items or open them or put them near the table. You are not allowed to say anything except "Yes", "No", "Me", and "Not me".

- -

You can move only when you have the scissors in your hands. You are not allowed to touch anything else. You are not allowed to say anything except "Yes", "No", "Me", and "Not me".

- -

You can move only when you have the bowl in your hands. You are not allowed to touch anything else. You are not allowed to say anything except "Yes", "No", "Me", and "Not me".

- -

Hierarchy of the Church

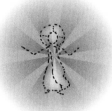

JESUS CHRIST

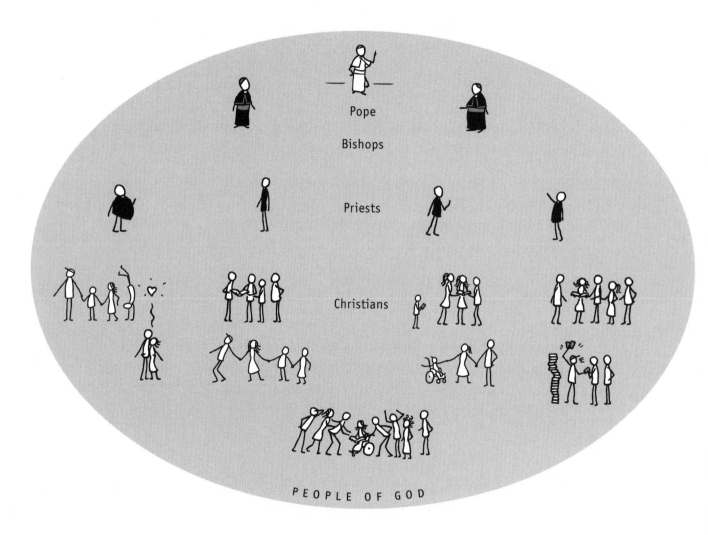

Pope

Bishops

Priests

Christians

PEOPLE OF GOD

The Eucharist—the Generosity of God

Theological basis

Around A.D. 300, the last and most brutal wave of persecution against the Christians in the Roman Empire began. Emperor Diocletian banned—on pain of death—the possession of the Bible, attendance at Holy Mass on Sunday, and the building of Christian places of worship. In a village of North Africa by the name of Abitene (in what is now Tunisia), forty-nine Christians were caught celebrating Sunday Mass. They were arrested and dragged before the proconsul in Carthage. When they were called to explain how it was that they had celebrated the Eucharist on Sunday, despite the strict imperial ban, one man by the name of Emeritus spoke up: "Without the Lord's Day, we cannot live."

Obviously he was talking, not about a free day in the week, but precisely about this: attending Holy Mass on Sunday. And in the year 304, these forty-nine Christians were brutally tortured and then executed for refusing to stop doing so. Their freedom, their physical safety, and even their lives were worth less to them than Sunday Mass.

Even today, in the third millennium, there are still some parts of the world where Christians are persecuted, though this is not (yet) the case in the West. Sadly, though, we can hardly say that most Christians attach much importance to attending Holy Mass on Sunday or, still less, to hallowing Sunday in the broader sense.

As human beings, we need a regular moment of rest—time to reflect and take stock. For six days a week, we may toil and celebrate, so on the seventh we ought to come to rest. Man is not simply a beast of burden; nor is he simply a party animal. Man is the image of God, and God rested on the seventh day after his work of creation (B → Gen 2:2): "So God blessed the seventh day and hallowed it" (B → Gen 2:3).

Again, man is not born to be a loner. All of us had parents, many have brothers or sisters and will later have a husband or wife and children. Most people have grown up in a family, to which they owe their ancestry, their tastes and attitudes. When father and mother, uncles and aunts, grandparents grow older, they become more frail—and often lonelier. We need to think of them as well. Beyond the family circle, we all have friends and neighbors—for man is a social being, a community being. If everyone were to have a rest day on a different day, then many people would be left very lonely, and our society would lose its cohesion.

Human community is the source of culture. And it is embedded in a cosmos, a surrounding nature. This nature has its own proper rhythms—day and night, seasons and natural cycles. Our culture likewise structures our time—with rhythms of work, of rest, of feasts and celebrations, and of worship. We do not simply live in a vacuum but are, rather, situated within a history. Traditions shape us, our cultural expressions surround us. It would be an impoverishment, indeed, a dehumanizing of man if he knew nothing but work and play.

The third of the Ten Commandments declares the Sabbath to be the day of rest and the day of God. YOUCAT explains the significance of the Sabbath for Israel (B → Ex 20:8–11, Deut 5:14–15; Y → 362), how Jesus dealt with the Sabbath (Y → 363), why the Church changed it from the Saturday to the Sunday, the first day of the week (Y → 364), and why it is now the Lord's Day (Y → 365). Attending Holy Mass is part of Sunday, for the Eucharist is the "heart of Sunday" (Y → 219).

Jesus himself associates the Eucharist with eternal life: "I am the living bread which came down from heaven; if any one eats of this bread, he will live for ever; and the bread which I shall give for the life of the world is my flesh" (B → Jn 6:51). And also with the resurrection on the Last Day: "and I will raise him up at the last day" (v. 54). For Holy Communion creates an intimate bond with Jesus Christ: "He who eats my flesh and drinks my blood abides in me, and I in him" (v. 56).

What happens at the moment when the bread and wine are transformed into the Body and Blood of Christ is a quantum leap. The Son of God has taken to himself the nature of man so that he can work in human history. But now bread and wine are raised up beyond their human context to become the new medium of a supernatural communication between God and man. Through them is mediated the salvation that was gained historically in Jesus Christ.

Let us remind ourselves of the story of the Fall: Adam and Eve reached out to the forbidden fruit. Holy Communion turns this event upside down—for now Jesus Christ feeds us. Previously we were thieves, but now we have once more become receivers of the gift. We must allow ourselves to be fed with the gift of redemption, just as young birds are fed, fed with "heavenly food". We recall the words of Holy Mass "... He took bread ... and, ... giving you thanks, ... broke the bread and gave it to his disciples." We are recipients of the gift of salvation. In the first Eucharistic Prayer, the old Roman Canon, we pray: "... that all of us, who through this participation at the altar receive the most holy Body and Blood of your Son, may be filled with every grace and heavenly blessing." This is a new kind of food, when from basic foodstuffs—which we are inclined to grab for ourselves and then throw away with equal thoughtlessness—the Redeemer is made present and received by us. But not only as a saving remedy, for through Holy Communion we ourselves become members of his Body. Every Sunday, when we celebrate the Resurrection, the Church is formed anew and herself becomes the Body of Christ, taken up into the love of God.

And this natural yet supernatural act, this uniting of earth and heaven, this reconciliation of man with God is a feast to which we are invited! The banquet that we celebrate is like a foretaste of heaven, a down payment on the "heavenly banquet", on the "Feast of the Lamb"... For more on the Eucharist, see Y → **208–223**.

LESSON

What Am I Supposed to Do in the Mass?

CATEGORY

Theme and objective:
Jesus wants to be close to us in the Eucharist.
Jesus is truly present in the Mass and especially in Holy Communion.

Preparation
- Photocopy the party invitation from Jesus (p. 80), and enter the name of each individual candidate in your group. Put them in envelopes, all likewise individually addressed.
- Photocopy (p. 81 or download at youcatconfirmation.com) the supplied refusals to the party invitation.

Introduction
At the beginning of the lesson, hand out the invitations to all the students, so they can open them and read them for themselves.

Saying No to the invitation
Have all your young people think about what they might write to Jesus to say why they won't be coming to his party. If your group is a little more creative, you can turn it into a skit. Each student can think up an excuse and phone Jesus on a cell phone to make his excuses. "Hi, Jesus, it's me. No, I won't be coming on Sunday, because ..."
If your group is not so creative or communicative, then they can each use one of the prepared excuse slips to decline the invitation.

Next, you can discuss together whether that is a good reason not to go to the party.

In your discussions, it should be made clear that such excuses would not be good enough if it were your best friend's party. A brief phone call (or prayer) is surely no excuse for not meeting him personally. The important personal message to us is contained in the readings and the Gospel, of course. If the question arises, you can also point out that there are usually several possible times for Mass, including Saturday evening and occasionally a Sunday afternoon as well, so that there shouldn't be a problem about finding time for it. All in all, to say No to the party is actually a sign that there is a severe crisis in your friendship and that you are really starting to grow apart. But that's precisely when going to the party could make all the difference ...

YOUCAT Session
Together read **Y → 219** "How often must a Catholic Christian participate in the celebration of the Eucharist?", and discuss it with your group.

Link
Assuming someone in your group has not already asked this question, you can lead on to the next part by saying something like: *"Now someone might of course say, I was at Jesus' party last Sunday, but he wasn't even there. And he didn't say anything to me ... Well, that's understandable. But actually we first of all need to know where our host really is when we visit him. And thank God, he has given us quite a few pointers to help us."*

Picture—"Where is Jesus?"
Hand out copies of this picture.

Jesus is present in the community
Now read with your group **B → MT 18:20** ("Where two or three are gathered in my name, there am I in the midst of them"), either directly from the Bible or else print out a card with this verse on it and lay it in the middle of the group. Discuss with them what this verse really means. Explain that Jesus is there whenever we gather together in his name to pray—and especially to celebrate the Mass. Have your group color in the assembled community and the priest at the altar on their worksheets.

Jesus is present in his Word
Place a card with the second quotation (from the Second Vatican Council) in the middle of the group: "Jesus is present... ." Explain to them that this is part of a statement by the Second Vatican Council, an important gathering of the Church that took place in the twentieth century and that was at the same time a preparation for the twenty-first century as well. Give your young people an opportunity, here again, to reflect on the meaning of this statement. The essence of it is that Jesus himself speaks to us when the Scripture readings and the Gospel are read out to us during Mass. Hence he is present in his Word. Get the candidates to color in the lectionary in a different color.

Jesus is really present in the Blessed Sacrament
Now read together the passage from **B → Lk 22:19–20** ("And he took bread, and when he had given thanks he broke it and gave it to them, saying, 'This is my body which is given for you. Do this in remembrance of me.' And likewise the chalice after supper, saying, 'This chalice which is poured out for you is the new covenant in my blood.' ") Alternatively, place the card with these verses on it in the middle of the group.
Once again, give your group time to think about what this verse from Saint Luke's Gospel actually means. If necessary, point out that Jesus spoke these words at the Last Supper, on the evening before his death.
Once you have established that Jesus is present in the Mass in the forms of bread and wine, go on to explain to them that in every Mass, through the words of the priest, a transformation takes place whereby the bread and wine truly become the Body and Blood of Christ, just as Jesus himself announced at the Last Supper. You should also explain that in receiving Holy Communion during Mass, we are truly close to Jesus—indeed, so close that there is no way we can come closer to him in this world.

Group work
Divide your students into small groups of about three members each, and tell them to reflect for ten minutes or so on what it means to them to be able to be so close to Jesus in the Eucharist.

Let each group present its findings. If necessary, explain that in this moment of intimate closeness to Jesus we can especially turn to him with all our concerns and that, if we entrust ourselves completely to him, we are taken up into his perfect love and ourselves transformed. And then we will be capable of living in the way that Jesus wants and also able to help our fellowmen.

Conclusion and prayer

Lord Jesus Christ,

in the Eucharist you give us yourself, because you want to be close to us.

Help us to understand this mystery ever more deeply, and give us the strength to respond to your invitation, even when we do not actually experience the desire to do so.

Amen.

LESSON

10

CATEGORY

What Am I Supposed to Do in the Mass?

Theme and objective:

Jesus wants to be close to us in the Eucharist.

Jesus is truly present in the Mass and especially in Holy Communion.

Preparation

- Photocopy the party invitation from Jesus from the materials provided, and enter the name of each individual candidate in your group. Put them in envelopes, all likewise individually addressed.
- Photocopy the party slips with the supplied refusals to the party invitations.
- Photocopy the worksheet for each student (also available at youcatconfirmation.com).

Introduction

At the beginning of the lesson, hand out the invitations to all the students, so they can open them and read them for themselves.

Saying No to the invitation

Have all your young people think about what they might write to Jesus to say why they won't be coming to his party. If your group is a little more creative, you can turn it into a skit. Each student can think up an excuse and phone Jesus on a cell phone to make his excuses. "Hi, Jesus, it's me. No, I won't be coming on Sunday, because ..."

If your group is not so creative or communicative, then they can each use one of the prepared excuse slips to decline the invitation.

Next you can discuss together whether that is a good reason not to go to the party.

In your discussions, it should be made clear that such excuses would not be good enough if it were your best friend's party. A brief phone call (or prayer) is surely no excuse for not meeting him personally. The important personal message to us is contained in the readings and the Gospel, of course. If the question arises, you can also point out that there are usually several possible times for Mass, including Saturday evening and occasionally a Sunday afternoon as well, so that there shouldn't be a problem about finding time for it. All in all, to say No to the party is actually a sign that there is a severe crisis in your friendship and that you are really starting to grow apart. But that's precisely when going to the party could make all the difference ...

YOUCAT Session

Together read Y → 219 "How often must a Catholic Christian participate in the celebration of the Eucharist?", and discuss it with your group.

Input and Link

"When we do go on Sunday to this party to which Jesus has invited us, then we do so above all in order to meet with Jesus himself. But to do so, we must of course first of all know where we can find him. And if you don't know your way around that well, it can sometimes be a little difficult.

"So, first of all, he is present in us, whenever we gather together to celebrate Holy Mass, just as he promised when he said 'For where two or three are gathered in my name, there am I in the midst of them' (B → Mt 18:20). And he is also present in the words of the Gospel that is read at Mass, since in the Gospel he speaks quite personally to each one of us. But he is present above all, and in an especially real way, in the Eucharist—that is to say, in the Body and Blood of Christ. And this is what we're now going to look at a little more closely."

BIBLE SESSION

Together, read the words of institution B → Lk 22:14–20. Distribute the questionnaires, and give every student around ten minutes to read the text again and fill out the form.

DISCUSSION

Have the candidates to read their answers in turn. Ideally, this will lead to a discussion based on their various answers. Probably you will also have to help a little by adding a few additional questions yourself. What should emerge clearly from the discussion is that Jesus really does look forward to celebrating with us; that he himself has instituted the Mass (Y → 209 and 210), and that in Holy Communion we can truly be totally close to him, because he is truly present under the outward appearance of bread and wine, now transubstantiated.

YOUCAT Session

Read the explanation on transubstantiation in YOUCAT (Y → p. 129–30), and discuss this with your group.

Next read YOUCAT Y → 216 ("In what way is Christ there when the Eucharist is celebrated?") and Y → 217 ("What happens in the Church when she celebrates the Eucharist?").

DISCUSSION

In your discussion, it is important for the following aspects to be made clear:

- In Holy Communion, we participate in the life of Jesus himself and thereby truly become the "Body of Christ" and, at the same time, are united with one another.
- When we bring ourselves and all our everyday concerns before God in Holy Mass, he also transforms us and strengthens us for our mission of transforming the world, in its turn, according to his will.

Conclusion and prayer

Lord Jesus Christ,

in the Eucharist you give us yourself, because you want to be close to us.

Help us to understand this mystery ever more deeply, and give us the strength to respond to your invitation, even when we do not actually experience the desire to do so.

Amen.

Dear ...

I'm writing to invite you to my party on Sunday. It's been a while
since we saw each other, and so I'm really looking forward to
seeing you again. Then we can finally get together and have a
good chat, I hope.
I know the music won't be altogether to your taste, but I promised Johann Sebastian that he could be the DJ this time. You
know what he's like. But all the same, I'm sure you'll be able to
manage it okay in the end.

Incidentally, Marcel is coming, too. I know you don't get on with
him, but I really like him. It's just that sometimes he can be a little, well, you know what I mean ... Besides, you don't have to talk
to him.
Anyway, I'm really looking forward to it, if you can make it.

Your Friend,

Jesus

P.S. I've also got something important to tell you, by the way! :)
More on Sunday!

Ready-made excuses:

The music isn't cool.

Marcel is coming, too. I can't stand being in the same room with him.

Sorry, can't do Sundays, as I'll be watching TV.

I spoke to you on the phone just last week; what's the point of my coming to the party!

You should have had the party in the forest. Then I'd have come.

I was at the party last year—surely that must be enough?

The party is simply too early for me—couldn't you make it a bit later?

Where is Jesus?

"For where two or three are gathered in my name, there am I in the midst of them."

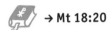 → Mt 18:20

Jesus "is present in His word, since it is He Himself who speaks when the holy scriptures are read in the Church."

→ Second Vatican Council

"And he took bread, and when he had given thanks he broke it and gave it to them, saying, 'This is my body which is given for you. Do this in remembrance of me.' And likewise the chalice after supper, saying, 'This chalice which is poured out for you is the new covenant in my blood.' "

 → Lk 22:19–20

Jesus celebrates the Last Supper with his disciples

Lk 22:14–20

What surprised you most in the account of the Last Supper?

- That Jesus had been looking forward to celebrating with his disciples.
- That Jesus knew he was going to suffer and die.
- That Jesus expressly commanded his disciples to commemorate this feast in his memory.
- That the broken bread is said to be his Body.

- _____

What seems to you to be especially important in this short account?

- That Jesus had been looking forward to celebrating with his disciples.
- That Jesus knew he was going to suffer and die.
- That Jesus expressly commanded his disciples to commemorate this feast in his memory.
- That the broken bread is said to be his Body.

- _____

What does this text mean to you personally?

- Jesus is also looking forward to celebrating with me.
- The Mass was personally instituted by Jesus ("Do this in memory of me").
- I can be truly close to Jesus in Holy Communion because the bread has really been changed into his Body.
- Nothing. It all happened two thousand years ago and is over and done with.

- _____

Update—Confession!

Theological basis

The Church of the first centuries took a very strict view about admission to Holy Communion. A person who was not yet baptized was not yet a "full member" and had to leave after the Liturgy of the Word. He was known as a catechumen, a trainee, an applicant for Baptism. Just as we do today when adults become Christians, so at the time the sacraments of Baptism, Confirmation, and First Holy Communion were administered together, one after the other. Anyone who was equipped in this way with all these graces was expected to live a spotless life from then on. Baptism had wiped away all sin, Confirmation had brought the gift of the Holy Spirit, and Holy Communion had brought close union with Jesus Christ and the whole Church. **Y → 226**

Anyone who committed smaller sins after this would try to atone for them with prayer, almsgiving, or fasting. But anyone who committed a serious sin, like murder or adultery, or someone who fell away from the faith had to undergo a process of public penance. He had to confess his sins in front of the bishop and the whole community and was only then admitted to the status of a penitent. That meant exclusion for years, sometimes even for life, from the reception of Holy Communion. Initially, it was possible to be readmitted to the Christian community only once in a lifetime. Often the penance was associated with severe social and even economic sanctions. In the early Christian era, there was a very strong sense that sin was a turning away from God and that a serious sin cut a person off completely from God.

Naturally, God loves every human individual, including the sinner. And Jesus has said: "I came not to call the righteous, but sinners" (**B → Mk 2:17**). We all know the parable of the lost sheep and how the good shepherd goes after it to save it (**B → Lk 15:4–7**). And we all know that Jesus is this Good Shepherd. But we should not misunderstand this parable. It doesn't mean: "You can make as much mischief as you like, and he'll still get you out of it." For this would be to forget two important aspects: 1. This Good Shepherd suffers for our sins; he has allowed himself to be crucified for us and for our sins. "The good shepherd lays down his life for the sheep" (**B → Jn 10:11**). 2. The sheep still has to allow himself to be caught. He has to listen to the shepherd and stand still. In this passage, Jesus has provided us with a very gentle, indeed, almost tender picture of the sinner. But do we not often behave more like the stubborn goats, who keep running away again and again, until they are perched on the very edge of the precipice? And are we conscious of the suffering of the Shepherd, who exerts all his energy, filled with love and concern, and reaches out to us just as we are on the point of plunging down?

This is what is meant by separating ourselves from God through grave sins—the fact that we persist in them, that we keep on running away from him until it is simply too late. For there is one thing that should also be clear to us, namely, that the story of the lost sheep would not have worked if it had remained in the sheepfold. Part of this story is about our freedom. The freedom to run away. Jesus won't throw a net over us to catch us. He doesn't have a stun gun. We are the ones who have to face up to it. This facing up to our sins is confession.

We must confess all serious sins. **Y → 233**

We must confess them before we receive Holy Communion again. At the very minimum, we must go to confession at least once a year. **Y → 234**

Serious sins are serious offenses against the love of God and love of neighbor that have been committed with full knowledge and with full consent.

Unequivocally serious sins include murder. Likewise abortion and adultery are serious sins, as is blasphemy: for example, swearing. **Y → 383, 424, 359**

There are many widespread misconceptions, such as: "I haven't done such and such, so I'm not going to confession. Children don't do that either, which is why they don't have to go to confession." Yet there is a good reason why the

Church tells us that anyone who has made his first Holy Communion must go to confession at least once a year, throughout his life. For the fact is that in order to confess properly, we need to have formed the habit of doing so. A person who has not gone for years can find it extremely difficult to go back again. He grows out of the habit of doing so, and the impulse not to go becomes stronger. Y → 235

We are not accustomed to talking about our faith, and above all not about unpleasant incidents or about our conscience. That is seen as extremely "uncool". The ideal "hero figure" we are regularly fed by the media is that of the rebel, who does what he wants. Situations of shame or regret are now found only at the level of what is or is not acceptable in society. For the most part, people have forgotten the fact that we are easily influenced by moods or fashions, by media pronouncements, and by chance. We tend to inhale the atmosphere of "what other people do or don't do" and blow it in other people's faces as though it were completely self-evident. We absorb it, perhaps, from some newscaster, television show host, or some other prominent personality. It soon gets taken up and parroted by other people around us, and very soon we, too, start to think, "everybody says that ...", or "now we have to ...", or "I'm not supposed to ...". It is easy to see that in this way our conscience is not being formed according to God's laws.

And so we need to practice the things that will help us stay close to God. Needless to say, most of us tend to think we are quite innocent. But that is not true: "If we say we have no sin, we deceive ourselves, and the truth is not in us" (B → 1 Jn 1,8). Even an accumulation of small sins can draw us away from the truth over time, can drive us away from God. Anyone who sits down with the aim of preparing to make a confession, some months after the last confession, will always remember something. And an examination of conscience can also help us to sharpen our conscience, to inspect carefully how we are living, what we are thinking, whether we truly believe.

We should get away from the habit of only looking to see if we have committed spectacular sins or abominable crimes. It is not without reason that pride, avarice, envy, anger, unchastity, gluttony, and sloth are called capital sins.

Anyone who examines his life for signs of these sins—they are called "capital sins" because they lead to others—will find bad habits, or so-called vices, that are derived from them.

- Do I tend to look on those who disagree with me as idiots?
- Am I always wanting to have what others around me have?
- Am I glad when someone who has more than I do suddenly finds himself in difficulties?
- Do I get grumpy when I don't get my own way?

In the Student's Confirmation book there is a good examination of conscience (pages 99–101). Other resources are available at www.youcatconfirmation.com.

LESSON
11

CATEGORY
🔥 🔥 🔥

Confession—What to Do with My Sins?

Theme and objective:
In confession we come back to God after having distanced ourselves from him through sin.

Preparation
- Get the Jenga game or a similar game involving a stacked tower.
- Photocopy the worksheets illustrating the parable of the prodigal son (pp. 91–93 or at youcat confirmation.com). If you want to use colored cloths as well, then don't forget to include them.

Introduction
Play a game of Jenga with your students. Or you can play two or three if you have sufficient time.

Link

Bring the game to an end, and point out that in our relationship with God we can also destroy everything all at once if we even only briefly decide to have nothing to do with him and simply take no notice of what he actually wants of us (see the lesson on sin). But thank God, if we do so, there is still a way of coming back to him. Jesus has explained to us how it works.

Parable of the prodigal son and the merciful father

Retell (or read aloud) the parable in Luke 15:11–32, and at the various points in the story lay out the corresponding illustrations. It's a good idea at the same time to portray the path of the prodigal son graphically by showing his path away from the father as a downward series and his path back to him as an upward progression again. If you would like to use colored fabrics as well, then you can use dark colors to illustrate the downward path and brighter colors to underline his upward path of return.

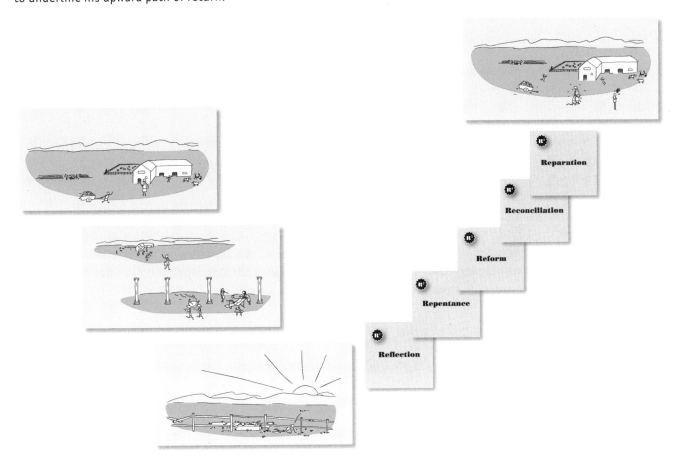

The way back to the Father

After reading the happy ending of the parable, take a closer look at the son's return journey. Explain to your group that we can identify five separate steps here that lead the son back on his homeward path to his father. Place the corresponding cards at the appropriate points on his journey.

Reflection
The son acknowledges that he has made a mess of things.

Repentance
He feels sorry for his behavior.

Reform
He resolves to behave differently in the future.

Reconciliation
He confesses to his father that he has made a mess of things.

Reparation
He is willing to work as a paid servant to make amends for his past behavior.

Input: Confession

Explain what this parable means for us in this way: "Jesus didn't tell us the story of the merciful Father simply to entertain us; he did so to explain to us something about God. The steps that the prodigal son takes back to his father are also the steps that we can take if we want to return to God after we have turned away from him."

Now go through the individual steps taken by the prodigal son, relating them to the sacrament of Penance. You can additionally read Y → **232** together with your group.

Reflection

Before making the decision to go to confession and so return to him, I have first of all to be able to see that I have distanced myself from God. And so I reflect on my behavior and on the times when I consciously acted in a manner different from what God truly wants of me. In searching my heart in this way, I will almost certainly find some form of examination of conscience helpful.

Repentance

In reality, confession has real meaning only if I truly have remorse for my sins, in other words, only if I really am sorry for what I have done. Otherwise, I may as well not bother.

Reform

It is also essential that I honestly resolve to behave differently in future. For if I can clearly realize that what I have done was not good, yet at the same time intend to do it again, then I must still be very far from repentance. The fact that I am weak and may possibly not succeed in my resolve is another matter. What matters here is the honest intention at this moment.

Reconciliation

Admittedly, this is probably the most difficult step. But it is vital that we actually speak our own sins out loud, because this protects us from trying to sweep them under the carpet as if they were not that important. After making this honest confession, we hear the words of absolution from the priest—and now our sins are truly forgiven! Moreover, God gives us grace to help us to resist sin in the future.

Reparation

Our readiness to make good—or repair—(at least symbolically) the material or nonmaterial harm we have done is expressed by reparation, or atonement. Usually the priest will therefore ask us to say a short prayer by way of reparation.

YOUCAT SESSION (OPTIONAL)

Depending on how receptive your young people are at this point, you can go on to discuss the following questions with them:

Y → **228** "Who can forgive sins?"

Y → **233** "What sins must be confessed?"

Y → **238** "May a priest later repeat something he has learned in confession?"

Conclusion and prayer

Who is a God like you?

Who is a God like you,
who forgives me my sins
and pardons your people their injustice?
You do not cling to your anger at me
for what I have done,
because you love to be merciful.
You will have compassion on me again,
and you will tread down my guilt.
Yes, you will hurl all our sins
into the depths of the sea.

You will show your faithfulness to your chosen ones
and your mercy, as you have promised to those
who believe in you,
from the earliest ages until now.
Amen.

(after Micah 7:18–20)

LESSON

11

CATEGORY

Confession—What to Do with My Sins?

Theme and objective:
In confession we come back to God after we have distanced ourselves from him through sin.

Preparation
- Get the Jenga game or a similar game involving a stacked tower.
- Photocopy the worksheets illustrating the parable of the prodigal son (pp. 91–93 or download at youcatconfirmation.com). If you want to use colored cloths as well, then don't forget to include them.

Introduction
Play a game of Jenga with your students. Or you can play two or three if you have sufficient time.

Link
Bring the game to an end, and point out that in our relationship with God we can also destroy everything all at once if we even only briefly decide to have nothing to do with him and simply take no notice of what he actually wants of us (see the lesson on sin). But thank God, if we do so, there is still a way of coming back to him. Jesus has explained to us how it works.

BIBLE SESSION
Together with your students, read the parable of the prodigal son and the merciful father (B → Lk 15:11–32).

Group work
Split up into two or three smaller groups, and give them the worksheet, "The prodigal son writes a self-help book". Your students should think about the five steps the prodigal son took toward reconciliation with his father and what titles he could give to the corresponding chapters in his book.

DISCUSSION
Let each of the groups present its results.

The R5 Method
Hand out the sheet entitled "The R5 Method", and introduce the five steps to the group:

Reflection
I acknowledge that I have made a mess of things.
Repentance
I am truly sorry about it.
Reform
I resolve not to do it again in the future.
Reconciliation
I confess that I have made a mess of things.
Reparation
I am willing to make amends for everything, even though it's probably going to be quite uncomfortable.

Input: Confession
Explain what this parable means for us in this way: "Jesus didn't tell us the story of the merciful Father simply to entertain us; he did so to explain to us something about God. The steps that the prodigal son takes back to his father are also the steps that we can take if we want to return to God after we have turned away from him."

YOUCAT SESSION—CONFESSION
Look at question Y → 232 in YOUCAT ("What must I bring to a confession?"), and discuss with your students what the R5 Method means for us in practice.

Reflection

Before making the decision to go to confession and so return to him, I have first of all to be able to see that I have distanced myself from God. And so I reflect on my behavior and on the times when I consciously acted in a manner different from what God truly wants of me. In searching my heart in this way, I will almost certainly find some form of examination of conscience helpful.

Repentance

In reality, confession has real meaning only if I truly feel remorse for my sins, in other words, only if I really feel sorry for what I have done. Otherwise, I may as well not bother.

Reform

It is also essential that I honestly resolve to behave differently in future. For if I can clearly realize that what I have done was not good, yet at the same time intend to do it again, then I must still be very far from repentance. The fact that I am weak and may possibly not succeed in my resolve is another matter. What matters here is the honest intention at this moment.

Reconciliation

Admittedly, this is probably the most difficult step. But it is vital that we actually speak our own sins out loud, because this protects us from trying to sweep them under the carpet as though they were not that important. After making this honest confession, we hear the words of absolution from the priest—and now our sins are truly forgiven!

Reparation

Our readiness to make good—or repair—(at least symbolically) the material or nonmaterial harm we have done is expressed by reparation, or atonement. Usually, the priest will therefore ask us to say a short prayer by way of reparation.

YOUCAT SESSION—CONFESSION II

After this you can go on to read and discuss the following YOUCAT questions with them: Y → 228 ("Who can forgive sins?") and Y → 233 ("What sins must be confessed?"). Your candidates will probably also be interested in hearing the following question as well: Y → 238 ("May a priest later repeat something he has learned in confession?").

Conclusion and prayer

Who is a God like you?

Who is a God like you,
who forgives me my sins
and pardons your people their injustice?
You do not cling to your anger at me
for what I have done,
because you love to be merciful.
You will have compassion on me again,
and you will tread down my guilt.
Yes, you will hurl all our sins
into the depths of the sea.
You will show your faithfulness to your chosen ones
and your mercy, as you have promised to those
who believe in you,
from the earliest ages until now.
Amen.

after MICAH 7,18–20

Reflection

Repentance

Reform

Reconciliation

Reparation

For notes

Please don't write on or mark this section.

One year later, the prodigal son writes a self-help book, based on his own life experience: *How to Get Yourself out of Any Mess—Five Simple Steps for a Better Life*

Try this: Think about which five steps the prodigal son actually took to be reconciled with the Father and how he might name the corresponding five chapters in his book.

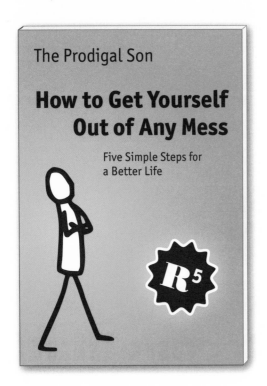

The Prodigal Son

How to Get Yourself Out of Any Mess

Five Simple Steps for a Better Life

R⁵

Reflection
I acknowledge that I have made a mess of things.

Repentance
I am truly sorry about it.

Reform
I resolve not to do it again in the future.

Reconciliation
I confess that I have made a mess of things.

Reparation
I am willing to make amends for everything, even though it's probably going to be quite uncomfortable.

Freely available any time, in your own or any other parish, local convent, or community!

SPECIAL EVENT

B

CATEGORY

An Evening of Reconciliation

Your Confirmation candidates need to prepare for their Confirmation by going to confession. So they can "wipe the slate clean", so to speak, before receiving this sacrament. In order to forestall some of the typical problems with confession, we suggest you arrange a special Reconciliation session for your young people.

ORGANIZATIONAL PREPARATION

Have different priests available
Get together a suitable group of priests for the session. It is important for the young people to have the possibility to choose between various confessors. It's also important to have at least one priest available who is not personally known to the candidates.

Offer a variety of outward forms
Make a variety of different environments available for confession. It is a good idea to accommodate the different characters of the young people by offering the sacrament both in the form of a more informal, face-to-face conversation with the priest as well as in the more traditional setting of the confessional.

Use lighting to create the right atmosphere

Try and create a quiet and contemplative atmosphere inside the church. You could maybe use a couple of colored spotlights for this, so as to illuminate individual columns inside the church with color. Your local or diocesan Catholic youth office might be able to help you here and may possibly lend you these. You might also illuminate the church with candles and tea lights, in order to create a "warm" atmosphere. (You should probably discuss this with the pastor first.)

Music and prayer

Organize a few musicians to accompany the evening musically. Modern worship music would be appropriate here. Interspersed with the music, you could have readings of individual prayers or meditations, for example, those from the YOUCAT Youth Prayer Book.

The musical accompaniment also has the practical advantage of providing a degree of "background noise", so that the candidates don't have to fear that someone might overhear their confession.

PREPARING THE CANDIDATES

You should already have discussed the essence of the topic of "confession" in advance with your candidates. Make sure they each have a copy of the accompanying YOUCAT Confession Guide, and discuss with them in advance what happens in the confessional. The Confession Guide comprises the examination of conscience and the introduction to confession on the following pages. By copying both sides, you have the front and back pages of this flyer for the candidates. You can then fold it in such a way that the YOUCAT heading becomes the title page of the whole leaflet.

Obligation to attend

In order to avoid a situation in which those young people who do wish to go to confession are made to feel exposed (As in "Aha, he must have a whole load of things to confess!"), you should make it obligatory for everyone in your group to attend the evening and speak with a priest.

It is important here to make it quite clear to the candidates themselves that no one can be compelled to make a confession of sins, since this can only be a voluntary action. If anyone doesn't want to confess, he must nonetheless attend the evening and speak with a priest and explain to him why he does not want to do so. The priests involved should be prepared in advance to deal with this possibility.

THE EVENING ITSELF

To start the evening, it is a good idea to begin with a short prayer and then sing a hymn together. If you have any other important organizational details to announce, this is the time to do it.

Introducing the priests

After this you should (briefly!) introduce the priests, so that the young people can form some sort of first impression of them. At the same time, you should also explain where in the church they will be stationed to administer the sacrament of Reconciliation.

Keeping to a set time framework

The whole evening should keep to a clear time frame, so that the candidates can all go home after the official end of the session. However, if any of the young people would like to stay on outside this time frame to make their confession, they should of course be able to do so. If the total number of candidates is so large that for practical reasons they cannot all confess on the same evening, then the program should simply be extended to two or more evenings.

If my heart often seems empty when I pray, that's no sin.
But it is a sin if I think I don't need to pray or if I don't even take the trouble to open my heart to God and listen for his voice.

If I am sometimes unsure of my faith, that's no sin.
But it is a sin if I withdraw from the community of believers, if I regularly refuse to take part in their worship, or if I think earthly things more important than heavenly ones.

If I make plans for my life, that's no sin.
But it is a sin if my faith in God plays no part in them, if I no longer care about the fact that my life each day lies in his hands.

TRANSLATED FROM THE GERMAN "SÜNDE IST … DIE LIEBE LEUGNEN", ED. BERNHARD RIEDL (ARCHDIOCESE OF COLOGNE, 2008).

If I experience sexual desires and impulses, that's no sin.
But it is a sin if I give way to my impulses or use others to satisfy my desires.

If I find it hard to like some people, that's no sin.
But it is a sin if I treat them as though they were not God's beloved children every bit as much as I am.

If I criticize other people, that's not necessarily a sin.
But it is a sin if I do so hastily or without charity or if I thereby demean or injure other people.

If feelings of envy, malice, or anger rise up within me, that's not in itself a sin.
But it is a sin if I do not try to overcome these feelings but, instead, let my actions be influenced by them.

If I talk about others, that's no sin.
But it is a sin if I gossip about others or say mean or spiteful things about them.

If I keep silent in situations of conflict, that's no sin.
But it is a sin if I keep silent when others are being disparaged, slandered, or lied about.

If I get into arguments, that's not necessarily a sin.
But it is a sin if I pick a quarrel, don't listen to others, don't try to understand them, or am unwilling to make peace.

The point about confession is for you to wipe the slate clean with God. So you need to take a look at yourself and your life and think about the things that stand between you and God. Now is the time to clear away these obstacles once and for all. The examination of conscience below may help you to take an honest look at yourself and your relationship to God:

If I enjoy the good things of life, that's no sin;
but it is a sin if I make them into my god and try to get hold of them at all costs.

If I want to earn a decent wage, that's no sin.
But it is a sin if I make wealth my one and only aim. And if I'm unwilling to share and have compassion for others for fear of missing out on life.

If I insist on my rights, that's no sin.
But it is a sin if I abuse these rights, if I become inconsiderate and hardhearted or disrespect the rights of others.

YOUR YOUCAT CONFESSION GUIDE

ORIGINAL YOUCAT CONFESSION GUIDE

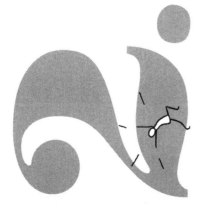

So now we get down to the nitty-gritty: The moment has come when you are going to allow God to do a spring cleaning of your heart. And the more honestly you let this happen, the clearer and more mature your faith will become. This is how it happens:

You go into the confession booth or the confession room.

The priest welcomes you.

You make the Sign of the Cross and say "In the name of the Father, and of the Son, and of the Holy Spirit. Amen."

The priest may now say a short prayer.

You respond to it by saying "Amen".

You can start your confession by telling the priest when you last went to confession:

"It is about ... weeks/months since my last confession." This helps the priest form an idea of your personal situation.
After this you can say the things you want to confess. If you're not sure about anything during your confession, you can always ask the priest, who will help and advise you.

You can conclude your confession by saying something like: *"I am sorry for all these things, and I want to make a fresh start with Jesus."*

The priest will now give a few words of advice as to how to avoid these sins and do better in the future.

The priest will give you a simple task to do, usually a prayer, as a sign of penance.

Finally, **the priest** will speak the wonderful words of absolution, which free you from your sins:

God the Father of mercies, through the death and Resurrection of his Son has reconciled the world to himself and sent the Holy Spirit among us for the forgiveness of sins; through the ministry of the Church may God give you pardon and peace, and I absolve you from your sins in the name of the Father, and of the Son, and of the Holy Spirit.

You make the Sign of the Cross again during these final words and respond. *"Amen".*

The priest says: *"Your sins are forgiven you. Go in peace."*

You respond *"Amen".*

After your confession, you can remain in the church for a while, to say a silent prayer and thank God in your own words for his forgiveness.

12 What Happens in Confirmation?

You can see it happen many times on the football field, when the trainer sends on a new young player for the first time. Y → 203

So it is with the playing field of life—sooner or later we all have to go out there. Though just how soon can vary. Many a young girl has had to take on responsibility at a very early age and look after her little brothers and sisters. A kid of fourteen can already begin an apprenticeship, while a high school student who finishes school four years later and then goes on to college doesn't really start to feel ready to take on responsibility until well into his twenties, and with a university degree in hand. When it comes to the sacrament of Confirmation, we speak of "spiritual maturity". Being confirmed is a sign that I am no longer a child but a young adult.

Now it is a matter of making the grace of Baptism fully valid in our lives. The confirmand says Yes to God, Yes to the Holy Spirit. He consciously and freely accepts for himself the grace of Baptism. That is not to say, of course, that he has been living without the Holy Spirit; for he has received Baptism and made his first Holy Communion. But this deliberate and conscious receiving of the Holy Spirit is something we have already seen in the New Testament. Jesus, in his divinity, is already by nature fully endowed with the power of the Holy Spirit, yet he nonetheless allows himself to be baptized in the River Jordan by John—and the Spirit of God descends upon him, and the voice of the Father says Yes to Jesus, his Son.

This reciprocal Yes takes place in Confirmation. It is like an indissoluble contract and marks us with an indelible seal—one that we can receive only once and that marks the individual forever as a Christian—a contract for all eternity. Y → 205

After the Baptism in the Jordan, something happens with Jesus: he begins his public mission. So it is, likewise, with the apostles at Pentecost: after the Holy Spirit has come upon them, they go out and begin to proclaim the gospel message. We describe this as the "birthday" of the Church. Y → 202

Now the Confirmation candidate is sent out in just the same way. He, too, has a share in the mission of the Son, given by the Father, and in the mission of the Church. The Church sees every Christian as a warrior. She wants to see the individual bear witness to the love of God. But the Church herself would not be capable of remaining true to Christ were it not that she, too, has been given his Spirit.

This Holy Spirit is what each individual Christian receives in Baptism. The candidate for Confirmation now freely says Yes to God. Confirmation completes the work of the Holy Spirit. Who is the Holy Spirit? Christians believe in a triune God—Father, Son, and Spirit. The Spirit unites Father and Son in love. Into this communion of love we are now permitted, as Christians, to enter. Hence, Confirmation unites the baptized Christian even more intimately with the Church. He receives the Holy Spirit to be strengthened (in Latin, *confirmatio*) and now becomes a Christian in the fullest sense. That is why young people also receive Confirmation when they begin to interact more strongly, outwardly, within the wider community.

But the effect of Confirmation does not depend ultimately on the maturity of the individual. For it is God himself who acts in this sacrament.

What actually happens in Confirmation? Let us explain, first of all, in some detail the actual rite of Confirmation and, then, describe how it unfolds. First, then, the rite of Confirmation and its significance:

Renewal of baptismal vows and profession of faith
You declare your Yes to God and your No to evil. You profess your faith before your bishop and before the assembled community. In the same way, after Confirmation, you should courageously stand up for your faith.

Extending the hands

The apostles themselves stretched out their hands when they bestowed the sacrament of Confirmation, the gift of the Holy Spirit. In making this gesture, the bishop is calling on God to send the Holy Spirit on the confirmands. He invokes this Spirit according to the seven gifts of the Holy Spirit: "the Spirit of wisdom and understanding, the spirit of right judgment and courage, the spirit of knowledge and reverence ... the spirit of wonder and awe in your presence".

The anointing with chrism

Chrism is a consecrated healing oil made of olive oil and perfumed with balsam. Both in the Bible and in the ancient world, oil has been a sign of abundance and joy, which cleanses, nourishes, heals, and soothes pain. Oil makes us beautiful, healthy, and strong. Chrism is specially consecrated by the bishop, once a year—in the so-called Chrism Mass, during Holy Week.

- 🔥 The anointing with chrism is a feature of Baptism, Confirmation, and ordination to the priesthood.
- 🔥 The anointing with holy chrism is a sign of consecration. Already in the Old Testament kings were anointed. Jesus was also anointed; that is why his name is "Christ" = the anointed one, for "God has anointed him with the Holy Spirit" (**B → Acts of the Apostles**). Hence we, too, as "Christians" are "anointed ones", united with Christ and filled with the Holy Spirit, so that our lives may exude the "fragrance of Christ" (**B → Second letter to the Corinthians**)
- 🔥 The bishop dips his right thumb in the chrism and with it makes the Sign of the Cross on the forehead of the confirmand. This is the mark, the seal of the Holy Spirit. No one can ever erase it; no one can ever repeat it. It lasts forever. A commercial brand mark can be cut out or forged; sealing wax can be scratched off or broken; an official stamp mark can be painted over; a tattoo can be lasered away. But there is no power in the world that can remove the inextinguishable mark, or seal, of the Holy Spirit.
- 🔥 This seal of the Holy Spirit means that you now belong entirely to Christ, that you have placed yourself forever in his service and will be protected by him at the end of time.

The sign of peace

The sign of peace is a symbol of the communion with the bishop and all the faithful in which you share from now on.

Now we come to the actual ceremony of Confirmation. It is a good idea at this point to go through the celebration of Holy Mass as well, just as it was first learned in preparation for First Holy Communion, and at the same time to remind the young people how they are expected to behave during the liturgy. Here, then, are the details relating to Confirmation:

The Rite of Confirmation

Within the context of Holy Mass, the bishop or his representative administers the sacrament of Confirmation after the Gospel.

First, the bishop gives a homily.

Then he receives the baptismal profession of faith (renewal of baptismal promises) by the confirmands.

The bishop asks the candidates: **Do you renounce Satan and all his works and all his empty show?**

The candidates answer together: **I do.**

The bishop: **Do you believe in God, the Father almighty, Creator of heaven and earth?**

The candidates: **I do.**

The bishop: **Do you believe in Jesus Christ, his only Son, our Lord, who was born of the Virgin Mary, suffered death and was buried, rose again from the dead and is now seated at the right hand of the Father?**

The candidates: **I do.**

The bishop: **Do you believe in the Holy Spirit, the Lord, the giver of life, who came upon the Apostles at Pentecost and today is given to you sacramentally in Confirmation?**

The candidates: **I do.**

The bishop: **Do you believe in the holy catholic Church, the communion of saints, the forgiveness of sins, the resurrection of the body, and life everlasting?**

The candidates: **I do.**

The bishop confirms this profession of faith as the faith of the Church: **This is our faith. This is the faith of the Church. We are proud to profess it in Christ Jesus our Lord.**

The congregation may now express its assent to the profession of faith of the candidates with a suitable hymn.

The bishop will now invite the congregation to pray: **My dear friends, in Baptism God our Father gave the new birth of eternal life to his chosen sons and daughters. Let us pray to our Father that he will pour out the Holy Spirit to strengthen his sons and daughters with his gifts and anoint them to be more like Christ the Son of God.**

Everyone prays for a time in silence (wherever possible, everyone should kneel for this prayer).

The bishop now extends his hands over the candidates.
All-powerful God, Father of our Lord Jesus Christ, by water and the Holy Spirit you freed your sons and daughters from sin and gave them new life. Send your Holy Spirit upon them to be their helper and guide. Give them the spirit of wisdom and understanding, the spirit of right judgment and courage, the spirit of knowledge and reverence. Fill them with the spirit of wonder and awe in your presence. We ask this through Christ our Lord.
All reply: **Amen.** Y → **310**

Now follows the actual anointing. A deacon or another helper brings the chrism to the bishop. The candidates come up, one by one, to the bishop, accompanied by their sponsor. It is also possible for a small group to approach the bishop. The bishop then turns to the candidate(s) before him. The sponsor places his right hand on the candidate's shoulder and announces his Confirmation name. Alternatively, the candidate himself may give his name.

The bishop dips his right thumb in the chrism and makes the Sign of the Cross with it on the forehead of the candidate, saying these words: N., **Be sealed with the gift of the Holy Spirit.**

The candidate: **Amen.**
The bishop: **Peace be with you.**
The candidate: **And with your spirit.**

It is perhaps not a bad idea to explain the central importance of Confirmation once again. It is quite possible that the bishop or his delegate may himself ask this question of the candidate. And nothing is more embarrassing than silence, when all the time we have been talking about mature Christians and courageous witnesses. And so check out:
Y → **203–207.**

What is Confirmation?
Confirmation is the necessary completion of Baptism.
Only when you are confirmed are you a fully fledged Catholic Christian.

How does Confirmation work?
Confirmation deepens your relationship to God your Father.
Confirmation unites you more closely with Christ.
Confirmation increases the Holy Spirit within you.
Confirmation unites you still more strongly with the Church.
Confirmation strengthens you, so that you can live your faith and stand up for it.

LESSON

Confirmation

CATEGORY

Theme and objective:
In order for Confirmation to take effect in us, we must be open to the Holy Spirit.
The candidates learn what takes place in the Rite of Confirmation.
Confirmation strengthens us in order to be disciples of Jesus.

Preparation

- Get a variety of different containers, a bottle or can, foil or plastic wrap and some cord.
- For the "action version", you will need a bottle of Diet Coke and a pack of Mentos mints.
- Photocopy the worksheet on "The Rite of Confirmation" (pp. 102–103 or at youcatconfirmation .com).

Introduction

Pour some water into the various different containers and seal them with foil or plastic wrap. Then ask your students to add some water from another can or bottle, but without removing or damaging the foil. Then, after a few attempts by your students, you remove the foil and add more water to the container.

Alternative "action version"

If you want to introduce the subject with a bit more fun, seal a bottle of Diet Coke with plastic wrap and challenge your students to add a packet of Mentos to it, without, however, removing or damaging the seal. Then, after a few attempts by your students, you can make the most of the occasion by removing the seal and pouring the Mentos as quickly as possible into the Coke bottle. Since the resulting fountain can gush pretty high in the air, and since in any case it can be very sticky, you should try out this version only in an open space and not wear your best T-shirt. And you will need to wash your hands and face afterward!

Input

Now explain to your students that in Baptism they have already received the Holy Spirit and that in Confirmation they will be sealed with the same Holy Spirit and thereby especially strengthened in their faith. Nonetheless, the Holy Spirit doesn't work against us or without us. That means that we ourselves have to be open to him. But if we really are open to him, then he can work and grow in us—like the water that was added to the containers. And sometimes he can be a source of real surprises—like the Mentos in the Coke bottle!

YOUCAT Session

Now read YOUCAT Y → 203 ("What is Confirmation?") together.

Worksheet: the Rite of Confirmation

Using the worksheet, discuss how the rite of Confirmation unfolds, and give the candidates an opportunity to ask questions. Maybe you can also tell them about your own Confirmation.

BIBLE SESSION

Together read B → Mt 28:16–20.

Input

Explain to your candidates that the mission of Jesus is also a mission for them. As Christians, they are the friends of Jesus and called to make all men into his disciples. Confirmation strengthens them for this task and also challenges them to fulfill it.

DISCUSSION

Discuss together how you can realistically help Jesus in his mission.

Conclusion and prayer

Send me

Whom shall I send?
Here I am!
Send me.

IS 6,8

The Rite of Confirmation

> The bishop: **Do you renounce Satan and all his works and all his empty show?**
>
> The candidates (together): **I do.**

After the negative, now comes the positive:

> The bishop: **Do you believe in God, the Father almighty, Creator of heaven and earth?**
>
> The candidates: **I do.**
>
> The bishop: **Do you believe in Jesus Christ, his only Son, our Lord, who was born of the Virgin Mary, suffered death and was buried, rose again from the dead and is now seated at the right hand of the Father?**
>
> The candidates: **I do.**

Then the bishop will ask you if you are really serious about the Church:

> The bishop: **Do you believe in the Holy Spirit, the Lord, the giver of life, who came upon the Apostles at Pentecost and today is given to you sacramentally in Confirmation?**
>
> The candidates: **I do.**
>
> The bishop: **Do you believe in the holy catholic Church, the communion of saints, the forgiveness of sins, the resurrection of the body, and life everlasting?**
>
> The candidates: **I do.**

Then the bishop confirms your profession of faith:

> The bishop: **This is our faith. This is the faith of the Church. We are proud to profess it in Christ Jesus our Lord.**

Now follows the invitation to all present to pray together. It is a little like that first Pentecost, when the infant Church gathered together around Mary and fervently prayed for the coming of the Holy Spirit. And as you know, moments later the tongues of fire descended upon them! So the bishop invites the whole congregation to pray together:

> The bishop: **My dear friends, in Baptism God our Father gave the new birth of eternal life to his chosen sons and daughters. Let us pray to our Father that he will pour out the Holy Spirit to strengthen his sons and daughters with his gifts and anoint them to be more like Christ the Son of God.**

All pray in silence for a short time. Fervently and from their hearts. It's best if they kneel at this moment, since kneeling is a posture of especially intense prayer.

Then the bishop extends his hands over the candidates. By this gesture the bishop draws together and gives voice to the profound prayers of all present. He uses the following words:

> **The bishop:** All-powerful God, Father of our Lord Jesus Christ, by water and the Holy Spirit you freed your sons and daughters from sin and gave them new life. Send your Holy Spirit upon them to be their helper and guide. Give them the spirit of wisdom and understanding, the spirit of right judgment and courage, the spirit of knowledge and reverence. Fill them with the spirit of wonder and awe in your presence. We ask this through Christ our Lord.
>
> **All respond:** Amen. (Which means: So be it; we ask this too!)

Now follows the actual anointing. A deacon or another helper brings the chrism to the bishop.

The candidates now approach the bishop individually, accompanied by their sponsors.

The sponsor places his right hand on your shoulder and gives your saint's name (or your name) to the bishop. Sometimes it is the candidate himself who is asked to give this name.

The bishop dips his right thumb in the chrism, places his hand on your head, and makes the Sign of the Cross with his thumb on your forehead.

The bishop addresses you by your chosen name and says:

N., be sealed with the Gift of the Holy Spirit.

You reply:

Amen.

This means something like:
Yes, so be it. I want this. I agree to this.

The bishop then says:

Peace be with you.

The newly confirmed responds:

And with your spirit.

So now you are confirmed.

Make the most of it! God is with you.

Last Page

Some resources are listed below. Additional resources are available at www.youcatconfirmation.com and www.formed.org

Video
Video: *Catholicism*, 10-part DVD series (available at www.ignatius.com)
Video: *Did Jesus Really Rise from the Dead?* (available at www.ignatius.com)
Video: *Footprints of God* series (available at www.ignatius.com)
Video: *Most—the Bridge* (available at www.amazon.com)

Faith Courses
Augustine Institute (www.augustineinstitute.org)
Liberal Studies Program (www.liberalstudiesprogram.com)
Institute for Catholic Culture (www.instituteofcatholicculture.org)
My Catholic Faith Delivered (www.mycatholicfaithdelivered.com)
School of Faith (www.schooloffaith.com)
Symbolon (www.symbolonrcia.org)

Literature
Mary Eberstadt, *The Loser Letters*. San Francisco: Ignatius Press, 2010
Peter Kreeft, *Catholic Christianity*. San Francisco: Ignatius Press, 2001
Peter Kreeft, *Jacob's Ladder*. San Francisco: Ignatius Press, 2013
Peter Kreeft, *Yes or No?*. San Francisco: Ignatius Press, 1991

Acknowledgment
The School of Prayer and the prayers on pages 88, 90, and 101 are taken from the *YOUCAT English: Youth Prayer Book,* ed. F. Georg von Lengerke and Dörte Schrömges, trans. Frank Davidson (San Francisco: Ignatius Press, 2013).

Thanks for their assistance with this Confirmation course

The authors wish to thank the following persons for preparing complete lessons for this course, which would never have been completed without their collaboration:

Florian Kopp
Richard Pfefferle
Florian Schmutz

For their important advice on the concept and method of the course, we wish to thank:

Simon Lipp
Michael Papenkordt
Barbara Müller

For the development of the theological basis and, thus, the framework and foundation of the entire course, our special thanks go to

Michael Widmann